Unchanging Truth
90-Day Devotional

BUCKY KENNEDY
LEA EPPLING

Unchanging Truth

90-Day Devotional

by Bucky Kennedy and Lea Eppling

Copyright © 2020 by Bucky Kennedy and Lea Eppling

ISBN 978-0-9826561-9-8

Printed in the United States of America by Lightning Source, Inc.

All rights reserved. No part of this book may be reproduced or transmitted in any form or by any means, electronic or mechanical, including photocopying, recording or by any information storage and retrieval system, without the written permission of the authors or publisher, except for the inclusion of brief quotations in a review or article, when credit to the book, publisher, and order information are included in the review or article.

Unless otherwise indicated, all Scripture taken from the NEW AMERICAN STANDARD BIBLE, Copyright © 1960, 1962, 1963 1968, 1971, 1972, 1973 1975, 1977, 1995 by The Lockman Foundation All rights reserved. Used by permission. http://www.Lockman.org
Scripture labeled NIV taken from the NEW INTERNATIONAL VERSION (NIV): Scripture taken from THE HOLY BIBLE, NEW INTERNATIONAL VERSION ®. Copyright© 1973, 1978, 1984, 2011 by Biblica, Inc.™. Used by permission of Zondervan
Scripture labeled NLT taken from the HOLY BIBLE, NEW LIVING TRANSLATION (NLT): Scriptures taken from the HOLY BIBLE, NEW LIVING TRANSLATION, Copyright© 1996, 2004, 2007 by Tyndale House Foundation. Used by permission of Tyndale House Publishers, Inc., Carol Stream, Illinois 60188. All rights reserved. Used by permission.

Cover design by Kim Radford www.kimradfordart.com
Text design by Debbie Patrick, Vision Run, www.visionrun.com

5411 Lawson Rd.
Gainesville, Georgia 30506

BKM Resources is a division of Bucky Kennedy Ministries

Introduction

Thank you for choosing this devotional to strengthen your relationship with Jesus. I have often found that God speaks specifically to the situation or season of life I'm experiencing through the devotional material I'm reading at the time. It's always such an encouragement in my walk with Christ. So, it is my prayer that reading these devotions will encourage you, regardless of your circumstances. I also hope that this book stirs your hunger for the unchanging truth of God's Word. While each devotion comes directly from a verse of Scripture, let them serve as mere appetizers to stimulate your taste for the meat of God's Word. Finally, I pray that these devotions are reminders of the Lord's incredible love. You never have to be fearful that Jesus will leave or forsake you. He loves you more than pen and paper can express.

In victory,

Bucky

Day 1

Jesus is Unchanged

"Jesus Christ is the same yesterday and today and forever."
Hebrews 13:8

There is an idea among some evangelicals that a change took place in Jesus when He walked on the earth. This train of thought teaches that Jesus gained a greater understanding of our sin nature by experiencing humanity, making Him less judgmental and more tolerant than His Father. However, today's passage tells us that Jesus is unchanged from eternity past.

The same Jesus who was present at creation, also walked the earth as a man. The same Jesus who was beaten, mocked, and abandoned, also died and rose from the grave. And, the same Jesus who turned a murderer into a missionary still changes lives today. Jesus is unchanged by time and culture. It's dangerous to believe otherwise. If Jesus Christ is not who He has always been, then how can we depend on Him to do what He has always done?

The grace we experience under the New Covenant isn't evidence that Jesus takes a more progressive view toward holiness or worldliness. In Him, grace and truth are perfectly balanced (John 1:14). He hates sin every bit as much as His Father. After all, it was His death and resurrection that established the New Covenant. Jesus didn't come to lower the standard or to widen the way, but to equip us with His righteousness for the narrow way (Matthew 7:13-14). New Covenant grace is not God changing His mind; it's God changing *us*.

That is the great juxtaposition of our Lord. He is forever the same, yet once He touches your life you are never the same. *"Therefore, if anyone is in Christ, he is a new creature; the old things passed away; behold, new things have come"* (2 Corinthians 5:17). Simply put, we are forever changed because Jesus is unchanged.

Day 2

Truth is Unchanged

"In the beginning was the Word, and the Word was with God, and the Word was God...And the Word became flesh, and dwelt among us, and we saw His glory, glory as the only begotten from the Father, full of grace and truth." John 1:1, 14

The word, "progressive" is used a lot these days to describe the notion that truth is evolving. Basically, it's the belief that people are more enlightened and intellectual today than in the past. Phrases such as, "Follow your truth" convey that what's true for one person isn't necessarily true for someone else. However, the meaning of truth cannot change, otherwise it was not true to begin with. So, if universal truth exists and that truth is unchanged, what is it?

Well, we established last time that Jesus never changes (Hebrews 13:8). Today, we see that Jesus has existed from eternity past and that He never separates Himself from God's Word. He *is* the Word and He *is* the Truth (John 14:6). Consequently, we find truth by looking to the One *"full of grace and truth."* As followers of Christ, we believe that all truth is God's truth. In other words, truth is divine in origin (2 Timothy 3:16). Therefore, biblical truth is infallible, absolute, and lasting. It does not evolve with time or cultural trends.

How then should believers respond to a world that rejects the truth of Scripture? The Bible calls us to *"contend earnestly for the faith"* (Jude 3). *"The faith"* refers to the truths taught by Jesus and the apostles.

This was in contrast with false teaching that had already made its way into the Church. False teachers still attempt to deceive by manipulating and marginalizing God's Word. The apostle Paul didn't yield to any perversion of the Gospel, *"for even an hour, so that the truth of the gospel would remain with you"* (Galatians 2:5). We are told to defend truth, not because it can be defeated, but simply because it's under attack.

While truth is unchanged, it certainly transforms and liberates anyone who believes. *"And you will know the truth, and the truth will set you free"* (John 8:32). Are you content to know the truth and freedom of the Gospel for yourself, or are you contending for the faith? The best way to defend truth is by sharing your faith verbally, then backing up your testimony with an authentic Christian life.

Day 3

Sin is Unchanged

"Everyone who practices sin also practices lawlessness; and sin is lawlessness." 1 John 3:4

People don't talk much about sin these days. According to progressive thinkers, it's judgmental to label particular actions as sinful. Even in Christian circles the conversation has moved to acceptable sins versus unacceptable sins. And the list of what's acceptable becomes more inclusive every day. The problem is — we don't get to decide what is and what is not sinful. Sin is unchanged. It's breaking God's Law by acting independently from the will and the Word of God.

At its root, sin is rebellion. Think about how sin was introduced into the world. Adam and Eve acted independently from God's will by eating fruit from the one tree that God said to stay away from. Now, eating fruit isn't sinful; but rebelling against God's instructions is. That single act also brought death into the world. Without sin, there is no death.

Everyone in the human race has participated in this rebellion (Romans 3:23). Over time, our culture has become so tolerant of evil that many children today say they've never sinned. We've become a society that *"practices lawlessness"* without acknowledgment or shame.

While Christians don't live lives of sinless perfection, sinful thoughts and actions should be the exception rather than the rule. As believers, we need to examine where we've followed cultural trends by tolerating what God calls evil. While we may slip into sin occasionally, we should never willfully step into it. When we disagree with God about what sin is or simply choose to go on sinning, we're actively participating in the rebellion. In which case, we are neither available or useful to God.

A believer cannot consistently practice sin without the conviction of the Holy Spirit. When we try to act independently from the righteousness of Christ within us, it produces conflict. That's why 1 John 1:9 is so incredible, *"If we confess our sins, He is faithful and righteous to forgive us our sins and to cleanse us from all unrighteousness."*

God hasn't changed His mind. He still views sin as rebellion against His righteousness. But He also sacrificed His sinless Son so that we would no longer be slaves to sin. As Major Ian Thomas said, "The life Jesus lived qualified Him to die the death He died. The death Jesus died qualifies me to live the life I now live in Him." Even though God's view of sin is unchanged, knowing Jesus changes our view of sin.

Day 4

Marriage is Unchanged

"For this reason a man shall leave his father and mother, and be joined to his wife; and they shall be one flesh." Genesis 2:24

God designed marriage for pleasure, for partnership, and for parenting. His definition of marriage today is consistent with His design in the Garden of Eden. Anytime we try to redefine what God has already defined, chaos and perversion are sure to follow. Biblical marriage is unchanged. Nevertheless, the same thing that infected Adam and Eve's marriage attacks the institution of marriage today; Satan's lie that God's way is not the best or only way. Our society has completely bought into this lie and we're paying the price.

First, God created sex and placed it within the confines of marriage. It's pretty clear that American culture is rebelling against God's design. For decades, the entertainment industry has depicted promiscuity as glamorous and liberating. Sex before marriage is now the status quo, which has led to an escalation of sexually transmitted diseases, abortions, and fatherlessness across the country. The sexual revolution has eroded the foundation of marriage and the home. Sex outside of marriage is outside of God's design because He knows it's harmful to us.

Our society is also redefining what marriage means. There is a difference between a legal marriage and a biblical marriage. Biblical marriage is between a man and a woman. God hasn't changed His mind. And contrary to popular belief, His Word does not adapt as cultural trends evolve over time. Yet, the biblical stance on same-sex marriage does not alter God's love for homosexuals. Neither should it keep believers from expressing godly love to them.

Finally, Americans are giving up on their spouses far too easily. Marriage is more than two consenting adults agreeing to live together. It's a lifetime commitment. Many people treat marriage like a contract that reads, "As long as we both shall love," rather than a covenant relationship that vows, "As long as we both shall live." As a follower of Christ, seek every avenue possible to reconcile with your spouse before throwing in the towel.

Our nation needs to heed the warning in Hebrews 13:4, *"Marriage is to be held in honor among all, and the marriage bed is to be undefiled; for fornicators and adulterers God will judge."* What worldly means is Satan using to infiltrate your attitudes towards marriage and sex? Agreeing with God's definition and following His plan not only protects you, it also honors and glorifies His Name.

Day 5

Forgiveness is Unchanged

"Peter said to them, 'Repent, and each of you be baptized in the name of Jesus Christ for the forgiveness of your sins; and you will receive the gift of the Holy Spirit.'" Acts 2:38

Some people say that if God doesn't judge America, then He will have to apologize to Sodom and Gomorrah. Remember though, God would not have destroyed Sodom and Gomorrah if just five righteous people had been there. He is always ready to forgive those who repent, just as He forgave the wicked city of Nineveh. Even today, God's forgiveness is unchanged. Repentance and forgiveness still go hand-in-hand.

People often don't repent for one of two reasons. First, they think their sins are too bad for God to forgive. Or, they think they are good and not in need of God's forgiveness. From a human perspective, we judge what's sinful on a sliding scale. What our culture calls "progressive thinking" and "tolerance," God still calls, "sin", just as He did with Sodom and Gomorrah. But God is merciful and His forgiveness is unchanged.

God's forgiveness isn't based on the depth of our sin, but on the price He paid for it. *"Or do you not know that the unrighteous will not inherit the kingdom of God? Do not be deceived; neither fornicators, nor idolaters, nor adulterers, nor effeminate, nor homosexuals, nor thieves, nor the covetous, nor drunkards, nor revilers, nor swindlers, will inherit the kingdom of God. Such were some of you; but you were washed, but you were sanctified, but you were justified in the name of the Lord Jesus Christ and in the Spirit of our God"* (1 Corinthians 6:9-11).

Did you catch that? The church in Corinth was full of people with dark pasts. The same blood that washed their sin away, washes our sin away. The same God who forgave them will forgive you. Even what we consider the smallest of sins required His sacrifice on the Cross. Forgiveness is available for everyone who repents and believes on the name of Jesus Christ. It doesn't matter how large or small the sin seems in our eyes.

There is only one thing that God does not forgive — the utter rejection of His gracious offer. The unpardonable sin rejects the conviction of the Holy Spirit, whereas repentance brings forgiveness and the gift of the Holy Spirit. Where do you stand with God today? You're neither too bad nor too good to receive the unchanging forgiveness of Jesus Christ.

Day 6

Salvation is Unchanged

"*And there is salvation in no one else; for there is no other name under heaven that has been given among men by which we must be saved.*"
Acts 4:12

The majority of Americans claim some form of Christianity. Yet less than two percent view their lives and the world through the lens of Scripture. So, most people are counting on going to Heaven when they die but they do not believe what the Bible says about how to get there. Nor do their lives reflect the life of Christ. Current cultural thinking can't change God's character or our nature, which means that salvation is unchanged.

First, salvation is still found exclusively in Jesus. In today's cultural climate, saying that Jesus is the only way to Heaven will quickly get you labeled as narrow-minded and intolerant. But Jesus is very clear in John 14:6, "*I am the way, and the truth, and the life; no one comes to the Father but through Me.*"

Also, salvation is still an act of grace and faith. Ephesians 2:8 says plainly, "*For by grace you have been saved through faith.*" Jesus illustrated this with the woman who washed his feet with her tears. After graciously forgiving her sins, He said, "*Your faith has saved you; go in peace*" (Luke 7:50). Genuinely possessing the saving faith of Jesus Christ compels us to profess that faith openly (Romans 10:9-10).

And salvation still has transforming power. 2 Corinthians 5:17 describes this transformation as being a new creation in Christ. Faith in Christ Jesus not only changes who we are, it also changes what we do and why we do it. All the things that are prominent in the life of Christ should be prominent in our lives — obedience, forgiveness, service, kindness, compassion, and sacrifice. Salvation is the life of Jesus in the life of the believer. The Lord then empowers us to accomplish His work through the indwelling of the Holy Spirit.

So, if you profess to be a Christian, how does your faith match up to what Scripture says about salvation? Biblical salvation is so much more than avoiding Hell and getting into Heaven, although that's pretty important. Salvation is Jesus coming out of Heaven and getting into us. Believing Jesus for the forgiveness of our sins is a starting place, not just a holding place until we die. Cultural trends regarding spirituality will come and go, but salvation is unchanged, and it always will be.

Day 7

The Lord's Promise to Return is Unchanged

"They also said, 'Men of Galilee, why do you stand looking into the sky? This Jesus, who has been taken up from you into heaven, will come in just the same way as you have watched Him go into heaven.'" Acts 1:11

The moment that Jesus ascended into the heavens, angels began to talk about His return. Two thousand years later, doubters and skeptics have increased with intensity. Yet the Lord's promise to return is unchanged. Although the time of His coming is unknown, we can be certain that He will keep His promise. Jesus' return is imminent.

Jesus spoke often about coming back, which is why the first century church lived with such urgency. They knew that Jesus could return during their lifetime, or at any time. So, why are we now at two thousand years and counting?

Some well-intentioned theologians explain the role immerging technology might play in end-time events; indicating we need to reach a particular point in human history to make prophecy possible. Some also interpret naturally occurring events as a sign that Jesus is coming soon. God, however, doesn't need perfect conditions, the aid of technology, or the laws of physics. Jesus' return is a divine promise that will be supernaturally accomplished.

The apostle Peter addresses the reason for the wait in 2 Peter 3:9, "The Lord is not slow about His promise, as some count slowness, but is patient toward you, not wishing for any to perish but for all to come *to repentance.*" God desires to seek and to save, not to seek and to destroy. The Lord's promise to return is unchanged because He desires to change the lives of those still living in sin, apart from Him.

If we truly long to see Jesus return, then we'll live in the righteousness of Christ daily. We'll get serious about sharing the Gospel with the lost, not only with words, but proclaiming the Gospel by how we live.

God has fulfilled every promise He's ever made — without alteration. So we can believe the promise of His Son's return with certainty. God has not changed His mind. Jesus is coming back down, the same way He went up. Believers should live with the expectancy that His coming could happen at any moment. Will you live as if it could happen today?

Day 8

Heaven is Unchanged

"Do not let your heart be troubled; believe in God, believe also in Me. In My Father's house are many dwelling places; if it were not so, I would have told you; for I go to prepare a place for you. If I go and prepare a place for you, I will come again and receive you to Myself, that where I am, there you may be also." John 14:1–3

Professing Christians generally agree that Heaven is a real place prepared for God's people. After that, ideas about what it's like can vary greatly. But Heaven is unchanged from what Scripture has always said. Misconceptions can be cleared up by simply reading what God tells us in His Word.

Many believe that we'll spend eternity flying around with harps. When a child dies, it's often said that God must have needed another angel. There's no scriptural basis for thinking that people become angels. Philippians 3 says that believers will be transformed to be like Jesus (Philippians 3:20-21).

Others believe that Heaven contains all the world's pleasures and luxuries without Hell's consequences. According to Revelation 21 and 22, Heaven *is* a beautiful, bountiful, and uncorrupted paradise; not because our flesh is indulged but because our faith is made sight (Luke 23:43). Without sin's curse, death and disease don't exist (Revelation 22:3a). So, there's no need for hospitals and cemeteries. Revelation 21:4 even says that tears of pain and grief will cease to exist.

There are also no strangers in Heaven. When 1 Corinthians 13 says that we will *"know fully just as [we] also have been fully known,"* that includes knowledge of believers through the ages. We'll enjoy relationships without jealousy or strife; living together in peace and contentment.

But foremost, Heaven is a place of worship because it's where Jesus is (Acts 1:11). Now, some people imagine eternity as one long, boring church service. Nothing could be further from the truth! In the Bible, Jesus was the person everyone wanted to be around; the guest who attracted all other guests. In Heaven, life and unmarred worship of Christ will finally be synonymous. Revelation 22 describes this constant state of worship in the presence of His glory, which illuminates Heaven continually.

Yes, Heaven is a place the Lord has prepared, but we must be prepared in order to go there. You cannot enter God's uncorrupted paradise in your sin. Progressive thinking cannot change the truth. To enter, you must allow God to change you by being born again.

Day 9

Send Me!

"Then I heard the voice of the Lord saying, 'Whom shall I send, and who will go for Us?' Then I said, 'Here am I. Send me!'" Isaiah 6:8

Few Christians are willing to write God a blank check, as Isaiah did. When God speaks, we often weigh the cost of serving against our personal preferences. This inner struggle can hinder our obedience, not to mention our willingness to step forward without attaching conditions. So, how do we develop a "Send me" attitude? Well, we need to see what Isaiah saw. His vision of the Lord in chapter 6 paints a stark contrast between God and humankind.

First, we need to recognize who God is. While it's true that God is a loving Father, He is also holy. *"And one [seraph] called out to another and said, 'Holy, Holy, Holy, is the Lord of hosts, the whole earth is full of His glory'"* (v3). The repetition of the word holy emphasizes His total separation from sin. We live in a culture that wants the benefit of God's favor and goodwill without recognition of what His absolute holiness requires — atonement, repentance, and obedience.

We also need to recognize who we are. Seeing God for who He is gave Isaiah amazing clarity about himself. *"Woe is me, for I am ruined! Because I am a man of unclean lips, and I live among a people of unclean lips; for my eyes have seen the King, the Lord of hosts"* (v5). His sinfulness, as well as that of his nation, was unbearable in contrast to the righteousness of the Lord. Today, many sinful thoughts and behaviors are no longer seen as wrong because our society has stopped acknowledging who God is.

Next, we need to recognize what God did. *"...your iniquity is taken away and your sin is forgiven"* (v7). Isaiah's confession brought the Lord's mercy and forgiveness. As followers of Jesus, our guilt has been replaced by God's grace (Romans 6:23). We don't need to dwell on past sin, but we do need to have an Isaiah 6 moment, when we recognize the holy God who mercifully and graciously provided the payment for our sins.

When you grasp who God is and what He's done, then you see yourself from Isaiah's perspective. This process begins in God's Word because that's where He reveals Himself. So, how much time do you spend alone in the presence of God? That's where we learn to say, *"Here I am. Send me!"*

(Excerpts taken from *Gracious Me! Exploring God's grace and what it means to be gracious.* BKM Resources)

Day 10

Being Gracious

*"The Lord is gracious and compassionate, slow to anger and rich in love.
The Lord is good to all; he has compassion on all he has made."*
Psalm 145:8-9

We've all met people who seem to say and do the right thing at the right time and in the right way. Being gracious, however, is more than being courteous and well-mannered. While we can be taught how to behave properly, being gracious is not mere outward behavior. Genuine graciousness comes from the inside out because it's generated by God's grace.

What exactly is grace? Well, most commentators agree that grace is the unmerited favor of God. It's how He freely demonstrates His goodness to humanity, even though we're undeserving of His goodwill. Psalm 145:8-9 tells us that every person receives some measure of God's grace, just by living in the world He created.

But the greatest expression of God's grace toward humankind is His gift of salvation. Romans 5:8 says, *"But God demonstrates his own love for us in this: While we were still sinners Christ died for us."* And Ephesians 2:8-9 reminds us, *"For it is by grace you have been saved, through faith — and this not from yourselves, it is the gift of God — not by works, so that no one can boast."*

Since we cannot live up to the standard that God's holiness requires, He graciously provided a way at Calvary. The holy Son of God died for sinful people. God's favor toward us is not based on anything we do or don't do, but is based completely on His love, mercy, and grace. It's this saving grace that transforms us; allowing us to develop the quality of graciousness.

This is where we have to get brutally honest with ourselves. Through salvation we admit that we can't meet the standards of God's holiness by our own merit, and we gratefully accept His grace. Yet we often require the people in our lives to live up to our standards and expectations. That's hoarding grace! It doesn't matter whether we're on the giving or receiving end — grace is an undeserved gift.

Would your family and closest friends describe you as *"gracious and compassionate, slow to anger and rich in love"*? Although demonstrating God's character is a high standard, that's what being gracious is all about! The quality of graciousness starts with an inward realization of God's grace that results in a new outward reality. Will you share or hoard that grace today?

(Excerpts taken from *Gracious Me! Exploring God's grace and what it means to be gracious.* BKM Resources)

Day 11

Growing in Grace

"But grow in the grace and knowledge of our Lord and Savior Jesus Christ…" 2 Peter 3:18

Have you ever watched a mature Christian remain steady in the face of an overwhelming challenge? You may have even thought, "I could never handle that the way she did." Well, that believer is living out the truth of growing in grace. Sadly, Christians often live as if their salvation is the sole reason for God's grace. However, grace continues in the life of a believer, providing what we need to speak and respond in a godly way.

Now, many of us have become quite good at the second part of today's verse; growing in knowledge. We listen to sermons and attend Bible studies, filling our heads with information about God and His Word. But if growing in the knowledge of Christ isn't balanced with growing in grace, then a prideful and judgmental attitude can develop.

Growing in the grace of Jesus Christ is allowing God to continually mold us into the image of His Son. How does this happen? Well 2 Peter 1:3 promises that God's *"divine power"* has provided everything needed for our sanctification. This power isn't an outward influence; forcing us into His image. As believers, we *"participate in the divine nature…"* by the indwelling presence of the Holy Spirit (2 Peter 1:4).

Spiritual growth, however, is not automatic — it requires effort. The nature that we nurture becomes our natural response. We grow in the grace of the Lord Jesus Christ as we diligently increase in qualities such as moral excellence, self-control, perseverance, godliness, brotherly kindness, and love (2 Peter 1:5-8). Responding as Jesus would respond becomes our natural reflex rather than a forced motion. That's because we're allowing His divine nature to respond in and through us. The result is a gracious and godly life.

It's wonderful to grow in our knowledge of the Lord, but don't forget to continually grow in His grace as well. Are you relying on the Holy Spirit daily; allowing Him to mold you into the image of Christ? God has already provided everything you need to speak and respond in a gracious and godly way. So, will you respond in your old nature or in the divine nature dwelling within you? Remember, the nature that you nurture will become your natural response.

(Excerpts taken from *Gracious Me! Exploring God's grace and what it means to be gracious*. BKM Resources)

Day 12

The Cost of Being Gracious

"What shall we say then? Are we to continue in sin so that grace may increase? May it never be! How shall we who died to sin still live in it?"
Romans 6:1-2

God's saving grace came at a significant cost — the life of His Son. So, it stand to reason that choosing to be a conduit of God's grace also has a cost. The question is, are we willing to pay the price? Well, Romans 6 helps us to know the facts, so we can act in faith and make a choice.

Fact #1: Believers are dead to sin (vv1-2). That doesn't mean we're perfect but that we choose who controls our thoughts, words, and actions. Just as a dead body is unresponsive, believers can choose to be unresponsive to sin. So, to willfully sin takes advantage of God's grace.

Fact #2: Believers identify with the death, burial, and resurrection of Christ (vv3-5). Baptism is symbolic of leaving our old self dead and buried. Just as Jesus was resurrected from the dead, we are raised to new life in Him (Galatians 2:20). Following Him daily means dying to self-interests; giving up our right to self (Luke 9:23). So, we can respond to others graciously.

Fact #3: We are freed from sin! (vv6-10). We are no longer slaves to sin; controlled by our old nature. You see, Jesus not only died *for* sin, He also died *to* sin — breaking its power. So, the only power sin has over us is the power we give to it. Choosing to act and speak in an ungracious manner is the spiritual equivalent of digging up a dead body!

The key to facing temptation successfully and responding graciously is to act in faith on the facts of Scripture. At the point of salvation, we claim Jesus' death *for* our sin by faith. And through faith, we daily claim our death *to* sin by choosing to be, *"alive to God in Jesus Christ"* (v11).

The cost of being gracious is dying to our own desires and choosing to live for God's desires. Are you willing to pay the cost? Will you leave your old self where it belongs — in the grave? His grace compels us to offer ourselves completely and willingly (vv14-20). After all, that's what dying to self is — yielding our thoughts, attitudes, and actions to Him. God will not force you to yield. The choice is yours.

(Excerpts taken from *Gracious Me! Exploring God's grace and what it means to be gracious*. BKM Resources)

Day 13

Speaking Graciously

"With [the tongue] we bless our Lord and Father, and with it we curse men, who have been made in the likeness of God; from the same mouth come both blessing and cursing. My brethren, these things ought not to be this way." James 3:9-10

The Bible has a lot to say about what we say and how we say it. Sadly, our words often lack the godly quality of graciousness. But not only do words have consequences; they also reveal our true nature. James 3:9-12 help us understand what speaking graciously looks like.

First, James warns us to avoid hypocrisy (vv9-10). Think about your typical lunch conversation after church. Does it ever include gossip about other church members or criticism of church leaders? Well, singing worship songs in church then tearing someone down at lunch reveals hypocrisy. James says we *"ought not to be this way."*

That kind of inconsistency is as unnatural for a follower of Christ as fresh water and salt water coming from the same spring (v11). Colossians 4:6 says that our words should, *"always be with grace, as though seasoned with salt..."* Salt is good, in measure. Likewise, speaking graciously is intentional. Even when difficult conversations are necessary, our words need to be measured carefully. Just as salt heals and irritates at the same time, too much rebuke (or even too much cheer) is too much salt (Proverbs 25:20).

Anyone who has swallowed a mouthful of ocean water understands that while salt is an excellent seasoning, it would be an awful fountain! Gracious words, like fresh water, give life and nourishment. They are refreshing (Proverbs 10:11).

James then points out that a tree can produce only one kind of fruit (v12). In the same way, our words should display the fruit of our resurrected nature rather than our old, sinful nature (Galatians 5:19-24). Producing both kinds of fruit is abnormal. The key is the root; the source. You see, refreshing words have a source just as surely as a freshwater spring has a source. We'll never consistently produce gracious words unless the Holy Spirit is our source.

So, are you producing any "old fruit?" Do your words go down like a cool spring, or are they choked down like salt water? A hypocritical, inconsistent tongue is a warning that something is wrong. Praising God but then engaging in gossip, slander, or criticism is unnatural and abnormal for a believer. Speaking graciously is the product of yielding our hearts to the Holy Spirit's control.

(Excerpts taken from *Gracious Me! Exploring God's grace and what it means to be gracious.* BKM Resources)

Day 14

The Source of Gracious Giving

"And God is able to make all grace abound to you, so that always having all sufficiency in everything, you may have an abundance for every good deed;" 2 Corinthians 9:8

The apostle Paul's writings say a lot about generosity and gracious giving. A major part of his third missionary journey was dedicated to collecting an offering from Gentile believers for the persecuted and impoverished Christians in Jerusalem. Although the church at Corinth quickly promised to give, they still had not followed through a year later. Have you ever been in a similar situation? Well, we can be generous because God, Himself, is the source of gracious giving.

God prompts His children to be generous over and above our tithe. As a believer, you've probably felt the desire to give to missions or a non-profit ministry. Even when we follow through, we may stop giving for a variety of reasons. Sometimes we're battling one of the enemies of generosity such as worry, greed, discontent, or misplaced security. We all deal with the "what ifs" of life. And let's face it — "what if" often becomes "what is." And nothing causes sleepless nights faster than financial difficulty or fears.

Still, God's grace enables us to trust Him with our resources. We can be openhanded because He promises to provide all we need to do everything He has for us to do (Ephesians 2:10). Did you catch that? God always has sufficient funds for *His* work. So, if something seems to be tying up our resources (time, energy, material wealth), then we need to take a closer look at whether we're engaging in God's purposes or our own.

When God prompts us to give, He either has already supplied or will supply the gift. *"Now He who supplies seed to the sower and bread for food will supply and multiply your seed for sowing and increase the harvest of your righteousness"* (v10). Since God is the supplier and the multiplier, there's no reason not to be generous! Gracious giving means that you trust God to do the math. He uses our gifts to do what only He can do; both tangibly and eternally.

Dependency on God is a spiritual workout. The more we exercise our faith by trusting Him to supply every need and to give as He directs, the more our faith is strengthened. So, is your security in God alone; or in God plus something or someone else? Are you generous with your time and your knowledge of Christ? Ask God to help you grow in the grace of giving (2 Corinthians 8:7). How will you exercise your faith by scattering the time, talents, and treasure that He has supplied to you?

(Excerpts taken from *Gracious Me! Exploring God's grace and what it means to be gracious.* BKM Resources)

Day 15

Graciously Forgive

"Be kind to one another, tender-hearted, forgiving each other, just as God in Christ also has forgiven you." Ephesians 4:32

Let's be honest. Some people and some offenses are hard to forgive. Yet God tells us that it's not only possible for believers to forgive completely — it's expected! Still, our selfish, prideful nature can get in the way of forgiving others as freely as God forgives us. But nothing displays God's character more than when we graciously forgive.

Since we are to forgive *"just as God"* forgave us, then let's really think about God's forgiveness. God's holy and divine nature forgives sin on the basis of Christ's sacrifice alone; His shed blood. While God's love for us is unfathomable, His forgiveness is ultimately an act of grace. So, if we are going to graciously forgive, we have to *"lay aside the old self,"* the sinful nature that was a slave to sin (v22). This requires a new attitude of mind (v23).

Romans 8:5 explains, *"Those who live according to the sinful nature have their minds set on what that nature desires; but those who live in accordance with the Spirit have their minds set on what the Spirit desires."* Your mindset is determined by which nature you live to please, and you'll live to please the nature on which your mind is set. We choose which nature we obey.

One nature pleases our flesh and seeks a personal agenda, while the other pleases God and desires His purposes. The mindset of the old self eventually leads to being an angry and bitter person (vv25-31). If bitterness takes root in your heart, then it will eventually affect your entire being and everyone in your path — not just the one with whom you're angry.

But remember, just as the old self was forgiven because of Christ, the new self forgives *in* Christ. When the old self is discarded, we're free to put on the new self; characterized by kindness and compassion (vv24, 32). Putting on the nature of Christ gives us the ability to love supernaturally, which leads to forgiveness.

Who do you have a hard time forgiving? The person who has hurt or offended you may not deserve your love and forgiveness any more than we deserved God's love and forgiveness. Will you be gracious and forgive him or her anyway? Remember, we extend God's grace and love when we choose to graciously forgive.

(Excerpts taken from *Gracious Me! Exploring God's grace and what it means to be gracious.* BKM Resources)

Day 16

Restoration

"Brethren, even if anyone is caught in any trespass, you who are spiritual, restore such a one in a spirit of gentleness; each one looking to yourself, so that you too will not be tempted." Galatians 6:1

If you set out to restore a dilapidated historic home, you would first need an idea of its former glory. Then you'd have to remove the "Condemned" sign, invest some sweat equity, and show that house some TLC! Well that's the same perspective we need on spiritual restoration. We're helping to repair sin's damage in order to restore someone to his or her former spiritual condition. Today's verse gives us the three keys to effective restoration.

First, exercise a spirit of gentleness, not passiveness. That means removing any initial thoughts of condemnation. Only then can you invest in that person by walking him or her through confession and repentance. The issue is not simply to control sinful thoughts and behavior but to consider themselves dead to it (Romans 6:11).

Next, recognize your own vulnerability. Remember, restoration rarely takes place from a position of superiority; it comes from surrender. It's hard to help someone else if you're not personally surrendered to the Lord first. Their sin may not be your sin, but be cautious. You can be entangled in sin yourself if you're busy looking at their sin in self-righteousness and pride.

Thirdly, bear their burden. Although you can't be another person's conscience, you can be a compassionate companion. Hurt *for* them and *with* them as they deal with the consequences of their sin. People often need someone standing in their corner, encouraging them, in order to be restored to a healthy relationship with Christ and with others.

Remember, the job of those who are spiritual is to restore the fallen brother or sister, not to point them out to others. Restoration releases the person who has been trapped by sinful behavior, whereas self-righteous judgment brings condemnation.

Has a particular person come to mind as you've read this? The test of your spiritual condition is not whether you condemn or condone their behavior from a distance. According to Galatians 6, you prove to be truly spiritual by lovingly and gently helping to restore that brother or sister in Christ.

Day 17

Self-Deception

"For if anyone thinks he is something when he is nothing, he deceives himself." Galatians 6:3

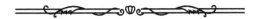

Few things are more hurtful than having someone we love lie to us. But the person lying to you the most often and the most effectively might just be you! A.W. Tozer once said, "Of all forms of deception, self-deception is the deadliest, and of all deceived persons the self-deceived are the least likely to discover the fraud."

Nothing aids self-deception more than comparison. When we compare ourselves with other people we tend to vary between two extremes: the best and the worse. The problem is that one extreme (the worst) creates conceit while the other (the best) can lead to self-condemnation. Both are deceptive because a wrong standard is in place.

The story is told of two rich but very wicked brothers. Both had wild lifestyles, using their wealth to cover up the dark truth. They attended the same church and gave large sums to various church-related projects. When one of the brothers suddenly died, the pastor was asked to preach his funeral. The surviving brother gave the pastor an envelope with a large sum of money. He said, "I only ask one favor. Tell people at the funeral that my brother was a saint." The pastor didn't see how he could make such a statement. The next day at the funeral the pastor said, "This man was an ungodly sinner — wicked to the core, but compared to his brother he was a saint."

While we chuckle at that kind of story, we also have to admit that it hits home a little. There is always someone who, by comparison, makes us look more or less spiritual. When we look for a lower standard by which to measure ourselves, then we're engaging in self-deception. Do you want to avoid the pain of self-deception? Then determine to use no standard other than Jesus Christ and God's Word!

Day 18

Examination

"But each one must examine his own work, and then he will have reason for boasting in regard to himself alone, and not in regard to another." Galatians 6:4

Scripture instructs us to examine our own work. This examination must be done correctly in order to live a healthy and effective Christian life. Of course, that means there's also a wrong way to approach self-examination. The standard we use for comparison determines whether we examine correctly or incorrectly.

It's human nature to measure how we're doing by comparing our lives to other people's lives. We can always find someone who, by comparison, makes us feel good about our work for the Lord or our moral standards. That standard, however, is faulty. Right examination requires assessing our work according to the standards in God's Word and whether we're being conformed to the life of Christ.

Healthy biblical examination provides crucial benefits: 1) Awareness. In order to see the need for dependence on God's strength, it's vital to be aware of our weaknesses. God's will is accomplished in God's strength. 2) Effectiveness. We engage in the right work through the guidance of Scripture. Busyness does not always translate to Kingdom effectiveness. 3) Excellence. Following God's standards assures that we do His work with excellence. Anything worth doing is worth doing well.

As God's children, our lives should be examined according to His Word, which is truth. The Greek philosopher Plato once said, "The unexamined life is not worth living." When was the last time you stopped to examine what you were doing and how you were doing it? What standard did you use for comparison? Any standard other than God's Word will render faulty results.

Day 19

Exhaustion

"Let us not lose heart in doing good, for in due time we will reap if we do not grow weary." Galatians 6:9

Being weary isn't just about being physically tired. It also involves being emotionally and spiritually exhausted. Weariness can cause a loss of desire to serve the Lord. The Bible doesn't ask us to work without rest, but neither are we to work without resolve.

There's a good reason the apostle Paul warns us about growing weary. As a matter of fact, here are three reasons. When we are physically, emotionally, and spiritually fatigued we are more susceptible to: 1) distractions, because we lack focus; 2) depression, because we lack purpose; and 3) defeat, because we've lost the heart to finish.

Many of us become spiritually exhausted because we forget to depend on the Holy Spirit and to rest in the strength of Christ. We confuse working *for* Jesus with trusting Him to do the work in us and through us. Weariness is often a sign that we've begun to work in our own strength. He gets more done working in us than we can ever achieve working for Him on our own.

Another way we grow weary is by doing a good thing; just not the thing we're supposed to do. Believers who are ready to serve often take on too many responsibilities. God may actually be calling someone else to fill one or two of those roles. Over time, the too busy believer grows weary. We don't have to muster up the desire or the strength to answer God's call. You see, the good works He calls us to do come with His equipping and energizing power.

Have you grown weary in a noble or godly pursuit? Examine whether you're relying on your own abilities rather than the guidance of the Holy Spirit and the strength of the Lord. Then make sure that the good thing you're doing is the exact thing He's called you to do. When you're engaged in God's work and relying on His strength, He will give you the heart to finish what you've begun.

Day 20

The God of the Impossible: No Situation Too Difficult

"Is anything too difficult for the Lord? At the appointed time I will return to you, at this time next year, and Sarah will have a son." Genesis 18:14

Attitudes like discouragement and doubt steal our peace and crush our joy. The God who defeated death is not intimidated by any circumstance we face. No situation is too difficult for God to handle. Just think about some of the seemingly impossible situations we know from Scripture.

The Israelites were caught between Pharaoh's army and the Red Sea when God did the impossible and parted the waters so they could cross to the other side. Daniel was thrown into a den of lions, when God did the impossible and kept the lions from harming him. Lazarus had been in the tomb for four days when Jesus did the impossible, and raised him from the dead.

There's another example in the Bible where God directly addressed the idea that a situation was just too difficult. God told Abraham that his descendants would become a great nation (Genesis 12:1-7). But he and Sarah were old and childless. When God's timing for a child didn't match up to their timing, they became discouraged to the point of taking matters into their own hands.

By the time that Abraham was 99 years old, complete doubt in God's promise had set in. Humanly speaking, Sarah knew it was impossible for a 90-year-old woman to bear a child. So when the

Lord said she would give birth to a son that year, Sarah expressed her doubt by laughing to herself, *"Shall I indeed bear a child when I am so old?"* (Genesis 18:13). Her laughter prompted God to ask, *"Is anything too difficult for the Lord?"* (Genesis 18:14). The birth of Isaac proved that Abraham and Sarah served the God of the impossible (Genesis 21:5).

Has something caused you to become discouraged? Maybe you're waiting on God to act in a situation that seems too difficult to resolve. Don't let doubt and discouragement creep in and steal the joy and peace of the Lord. Rather than think about what God can possibly do in that situation, dwell on the fact that there's nothing our God can't do! His answer might come in a surprising way and at an unexpected time, but our faith is in the God of the impossible.

Day 21

The God of the Impossible: No Promise Too Big

"For as many as are the promises of God, in Him they are yes; therefore also through Him is our Amen to the glory of God through us." 2 Corinthians 1:20

There are approximately 30,000 promises in the Bible. Think about a few of the incredible promises that God has already kept to specific people in Scripture. He promised Joshua and the Israelites that the walls of Jericho would fall, and they did. He promised Elijah that food would come to him from ravens, and it did. He promised the virgin Mary that she would give birth to a son, and she did. There is one promise, however, that was a game changer.

Even though they didn't understand what He was saying at the time, Jesus promised His disciples that He would rise from the dead in three days, and He did. Keeping His promise to conquer death and the grave made every other promise in the New Testament possible.

The great preacher Charles Spurgeon illustrated this point by describing God's promises like a check made out in your name. If you are without funds, it's not the fault of the person who gave you the check. In order to get what is promised, you have to sign the check and present it for deposit. In prayer, we can present God's promises (endorsed by our personal faith), obtain the blessing, and go about our Master's business.

So, if you are struggling with anxiety, then you can present Jesus' promise for His peace (John 14:27). When you're faced with temptation, claim His promise of escape (1 Corinthians 10:13). If that temptation gets you, present His promise to forgive confessed sin (1 John 1:9). Do you have a pressing need? Then claim God's promise to meet all of your needs (Philippians 4:19). Do you need wisdom for a decision at work or a difficult family situation? God promises to give wisdom liberally when you ask according to James 1:5-8.

If you have not yet chosen to place your trust in Jesus Christ for salvation, then God promises:

"That if you confess with your mouth Jesus as Lord, and believe in your heart that God raised Him from the dead, you will be saved; for with the heart a person believes, resulting in righteousness, and with the mouth he confesses, resulting in salvation" (Romans 10:9-10).

There is absolutely no promise too hard or too big for God to make good on. And yes, you can take that to the bank!

Day 22

The God of the Impossible: No Request Too Challenging

"Call to Me and I will answer you, and I will show you great and mighty things, which you do not know." Jeremiah 33:3

When we're faced with a seemingly impossible situation, we sometimes approach prayer as a last resort. Our minds can get so bogged down in what's humanly possible that we fail to remember that no request is too challenging for God. Consider a few examples from the Bible.

Joshua asked God to stop the sun from moving, and it stood still in the sky for a full day. Elijah prayed that it would not rain, and it didn't until he asked God to pour down rain three years later. After Hezekiah was told of his imminent death, he asked the Lord to remember him, and God added 15 years to his life.

In Jeremiah 33:3, God gives three specific reasons to pray. 1) Prayer is not optional for a child of God; it's a command. 2) God promises to answer when we pray. He reveals Himself and His will when we call on Him. 3) He will show us great and mighty things. God desires to show us things about Himself that the world doesn't think about; things they cannot even imagine!

However, we have to remember that prayer isn't some kind of magical way to get what we want. Consider a few other things Scripture tells us about prayer. The ultimate aim of our requests should be to glorify God (John 14:13-14). God often says, "No" because we ask with wrong motives (James 4:3). The impossible is possible when we ask with genuine faith (Matthew 17:20).

Michael Guido tells a story from early in his ministry. After preaching in San Jose, he and Audrey were driving to Los Angeles. Because the motel had cost more than expected, they had no money left for food. So, Audrey prayed, "Dear Lord, the Bible says, *'The Lord is my shepherd, I shall not want.'* We need ten dollars. Please give it to us."

Suddenly, a truck zoomed passed them then screeched to a stop. The driver ran to their car and said, "I don't know you, but as I passed your car something said, 'Give them ten dollars.'" He threw the money into Audrey's lap, ran back to his truck, and drove away. The Guidos sat in their car, crying and thanking the Lord.

Your challenging request for God is probably somewhere between ten dollars and making the sun stand still in the sky! But whatever situation you're in today, remember that our God is the God of the impossible. Prayer is not your last resort; it should be your first resource.

Day 23

The God of the Impossible: No Person Too Lost

"Therefore He is able also to save forever those who draw near to God through Him, since He always lives to make intercession for them." Hebrews 7:25

Have you ever thought that there might be someone who is so far gone, so evil that they are beyond redemption? Well, in 1979 Ted Bundy was sentenced to death for the murder of two female college students. During his decade on death row, he confessed to killing at least 28 young women. Then on the eve of his execution, Bundy said he had found forgiveness through Jesus Christ; a revelation that shocked and appalled many. Is it possible that God would offer redemption to someone as depraved as Ted Bundy?

Well, the Bible reveals that Jesus saved some pretty hard cases, such as:
- A woman who'd been married five times and was living with yet another man (John 4);
- A condemned thief dying on a cross (Luke 23);
- A religious zealot who persecuted and imprisoned followers of Christ (Acts 9)

When you stop and think about it, Ted Bundy had some things in common with these three. 1) Like the woman at the well, he was guilty of immorality. You see, the allure of soft-core pornography turned into an addiction to hard-core, violent porn; which fueled his numerous sex crimes and murders. 2) Like the thief on the cross, Ted was a condemned man with a death sentence. 3) Like the religious zealot, Saul of Tarsus, Ted Bundy was a murderer. Are any of these people too lost for God to save?

The change that took place in the life of Saul was so complete that it required a new name. Listen to how the apostle Paul explains his forgiveness and redemption, *"...Christ Jesus came into the world to save sinners, among whom I am foremost of all* (1 Timothy 1:15). The man who considered himself the worst of all sinners became the greatest missionary the world has ever known.

God's grace is abundant and available to anyone who recognizes their sinfulness and believes on Jesus for forgiveness. If someone has come to your mind as you've read this, then will you commit to pray for his or her salvation? If that person is you, then take Hebrews 7:25 to heart, *"He is able to save forever those who draw near to God."* God is able, are you available?

Day 24

Making Your Mark

"So teach us to number our days, that we may present to You a heart of wisdom." Psalm 90:12

You can live your life in one of three ways: waste it, spend it, or invest it. Today's verse challenges us to think about our purpose as we approach each new day. In order to live a meaningful life, we should consider a few things from the life of the apostle Paul, a man who sought to make his life count for eternity.

In Romans 15:16, Paul tells us that it's the grace of God that made him, *"a minister of Jesus Christ to the Gentiles."* Living a life of purpose means living life *on* purpose. If we aim at nothing we are pretty sure to hit nothing. A casual and careless person lives only for the moment, while the life lived in conformity to Christ lives for the service of others and the reward of eternity.

Paul wasn't successful because of his abilities but because of his availability. He often speaks of being dead to self in order to be alive in Christ. Paul was available to the Lord because his own selfish purposes were dead. He united with Christ in his death so he could fully identify with Christ in his life.

Paul was driven to do only that which fulfilled his God-given mission: take the Gospel of Jesus to people who had never heard it.

This godly ambition was fueled by a burning conviction that he would live eternally with the Lord.

Paul didn't fear the loss of this world because he knew it was not his home. You see, once you have found what you will die for, then you have found what you will live for. Remember this: what you spend, you lose; what you save, you give to others; and what you give to God, you will always have.

What kind of mark will your life leave on this world? The answer depends on whether your purpose in life is temporal or eternal. Live today in such a way that people not only know that you lived, but they know *why* you lived. Make it count for eternity!

Day 25

Beware of the Snare

"Keep me from the jaws of the trap which they have set for me, and from the snares of those who do iniquity. Let the wicked fall into their own nets, while I pass by safely." Psalm 141:9-10

Difficulties are just a fact of life because we live in a corrupt, evil, and fallen world. But many times, we find ourselves in a difficult situation because we've walked right into one of the enemy's snares. Merriam-Webster defines a snare as, "something by which one is entangled, involved in difficulties, or impeded; something deceptively attractive."

In Psalm 141, David asks the Lord to keep him from becoming entangled with people, places, and practices designed to keep him from glorifying God. Believers still face snares today. Satan and his forces desire to impede our faith and to make our testimonies ineffective.

These snares can harm us spiritually, physically, and emotionally. Many followers of Christ fail to understand that because they are deeply loved by God, they are also greatly hated by the devil. Too often, we place ourselves at great risk by underestimating our individual value to God and by overestimating our individual worth to the world.

Just because a snare has been designed for you doesn't mean you are destined to be trapped by it. Will you determine today to beware of the enemy's snares? Examine the choices you make and the companions you keep. Are you walking dangerously close to something that will entangle you, keeping you from honoring the Lord with your life? When we focus our eyes on Jesus, He orders our steps so that designed snares become defeated snares.

Day 26

The Snare of Our Words

"Set a guard, O Lord, over my mouth; keep watch over the door of my lips." Psalm 141:3

In the age of social media, many people post unguarded words about their lives or their opinions of others. There was a time when gossips and slanderers needed willing participants to spread hurtful and harmful words. Now they just need a keypad, and the internet does the rest. Our words can be a hazardous snare if we're not selective in how and when we use them. King David's prayer in Psalm 141 challenges us to choose our words carefully.

The T.H.I.N.K. test is a helpful tool for guarding our mouths and our posting. Ask yourself: is it true? Is it helpful? Is it inspiring? Is it necessary? And is it kind? If you have to start a conversation or post with, "I probably shouldn't say this, but..." then it's probably wise to stop and T.H.I.N.K. about it first.

President Calvin Coolidge was famously known as a man of few words. His nickname was "Silent Cal." His wife, Grace, told the story of a young woman who sat next to her husband at a dinner party. She told Coolidge she had a bet with a friend that she could get at least three words of conversation from him. Without looking at her he quietly retorted, "You lose." President Coolidge understood the value of using few words, and those being carefully chosen.

By taking time to carefully consider our words, we're less likely to say or post that impulsive thought. What would happen if you genuinely prayed Psalm 141:3 at the beginning of your day? Don't get caught in the snare of your own words today. Remember that *"Death and life are in the power of the tongue"* (Proverbs 18:21). Choose to yield to the Holy Spirit, allowing Him to guard what comes from your lips, and your keyboard.

Day 27

The Snare of Our Wants

*"For I know that nothing good dwells in me, that is,
in my flesh; for the willing is present in me,
but the doing of the good is not."* Romans 7:18

We need to be careful that our wants don't become snares. How? By examining what we want and checking that against the Word of God. Today's verse reminds us that our flesh is our biggest problem.

In the Garden of Eden, Satan tempted Adam and Eve to want what God said they couldn't have. As a result, sin entered into the world. We also see the effects of worldly desire fully on display in the life of King David. His sinful pursuit of Bathsheba taught him that taking what you want comes with a painful price. But it was a desire for godly restraint that caused David to pray, *"Do not incline my heart to any evil thing…"* (Psalm 141:4). David knew all too well that a desire driven by the flesh was a trap of the enemy.

Satan still loves to tempt us with our wants. As a matter of fact, he's become an expert at it. He works to manipulate and control us with the pleasures of the moment. When he's successful, we can't enjoy the abundant life that we're intended to live in Christ Jesus.

Of course, some of the things we want aren't evil in and of themselves. However, it is sin if we have to compromise God's Word or ignore the Holy Spirit in order to get them. Jesus tells us in Matthew 7:11, *"If you then, being evil know how to give good gifts to your children, how much more will your Father who is in heaven give what is good to those who ask Him!"* And Psalm 84:11 reminds us, *"The Lord gives grace and glory; no good thing does He withhold from those who walk uprightly."*

So, what's going on in your heart? Are your current desires driven by your flesh or are they under the control of the Holy Spirit? What causes your wants to be out of line with God's Word? You don't have to fall for the snare of your wants. Getting our wants under control is a matter of trusting God for everything we have. And having what you want is often a matter of wanting what God has already supplied.

Day 28

The Snare of Our Works

"Do not incline my heart to any evil thing, to practice deeds of wickedness with men who do iniquity." Psalm 141:4

The friends we choose often determine the places we go and the pleasures we seek. The cultural influences we allow into our minds have a dramatic influence on us as well. If you're not mindful of who and what influence your thinking, then you'll soon lose the desire for godly things. Left unchecked, you'll even grow accustomed to living by what your flesh desires. Those works of the flesh are a snare to your walk with the Lord.

In today's verse, we see that King David understood this. He knew that the people he associated with and the things he desired influenced him to live either a godly or an ungodly life. We also see his influence on his son, Solomon, who warned, *"Do not be envious of evil men, nor desire to be with them; for their minds devise violence, and their lips talk of trouble"* (Proverbs 24:1-2).

As people who claim the name of Christ, Christians should demonstrate His nature in daily life. Are we causing people to stumble by the things we do and the places we go? Or, are our deeds noble, honorable, and glorifying to the Lord? God is paying attention. Proverbs 5:21 tells us, *"For the ways of a man are before the eyes of the Lord, and He watches all his paths."*

It's not just the things we do in our flesh that are snares. Our good works can also become a snare because they offer a false sense of security. The devil convinces many people that as long as they do good deeds publicly then what they think and do privately is of little consequence. But remember, nothing is hidden from the Lord. He also pays attention to what's going on in our hearts and minds.

With whom do you spend most of your time? What books, music, movies, and television shows have you allowed into your mind? Are they influencing you toward righteousness or toward wickedness? Ask God to make you more aware of ungodly influences in your life. Choose to guard your heart and mind from anything unrighteous. Then determine to live each moment with integrity before the Lord. You see, for a believer faith is not just a part of life — it *is* life!

Day 29

The Beatitudes:
The Possession of Blessing

"When Jesus saw the crowds, He went up on the mountain; and after He sat down, His disciples came to Him. He opened His mouth and began to teach them, saying..." Matthew 5:1-2

We often confuse being blessed with being happy. Whether we're happy or not is usually tied to our circumstances, while being blessed is about our relationship with Jesus Christ. Jesus began the Sermon on the Mount with the definition of what it means to be blessed according to the promises of God. We know these twelve verses as The Beatitudes because He teaches us who we are to be, not what we are to do.

Blessing comes from within because of the indwelling of the Holy Spirit, but we have to appropriate those promises personally. The Beatitudes become a reality in our lives as we believe by faith that God enables us to live a blessed life. So being blessed is the result of being in a personal relationship with the Lord and maintaining that relationship rightly.

Now, when Jesus said, *"Blessed are you"* He didn't mean "untroubled are you." If we're secure and content in Him, then we'll also be prepared to deal with the troubling circumstances around us. A person is instantly and eternally blessed by surrendering his or her life to Jesus. At the moment of salvation, we receive the forgiveness of sins, we are infused with the righteousness of Christ, and we are granted eternal life in Heaven. We're blessed, not because of what we possess, but because of Who possesses us.

In the next several devotions, we're going to talk about how to appropriate each of the Beatitudes in our lives. As we do, remember that blessing is part of your character when you live in surrender to Jesus Christ; submitting your will to His will. The possession of blessing is found in the One who possesses you.

Day 30

The Beatitudes:
The Blessing of Emptiness

"Blessed are the poor in spirit for theirs is the kingdom of heaven." Matthew 5:3

Last time, we started a series on the Beatitudes from The Sermon on the Mount. We talked about the fact that we are blessed in Jesus Christ. Now we'll move into the specifics of each blessing, starting with being poor in spirit.

The crowd listening to Jesus that day was made up of all kinds of people, including those who were very religious. These people were working hard to prove their goodness and their religious superiority. They were self-righteous, defining their religion by who they were and what they did. Today, we think of these kind of people as being "full of themselves." Jesus, however, taught that we need to be empty of self. To be poor in spirit is to recognize that we have no righteousness in who we are and what we do, but only in Jesus.

This kind of teaching was foreign to the religious crowd. They thought the Messiah was coming to establish His Kingdom on Earth and that they would have a prestigious place in that kingdom as a reward for all they had done. But in this opening statement, Jesus tells them that the Kingdom of Heaven belongs to those who are empty of the spirit of self. You see, there's no room for self-righteousness when we're filled with His righteousness.

Jesus was teaching His followers to do exactly what He did when He came to Earth; He emptied Himself of His position, His possessions, and His power in order to submit to the will of His Father and to fulfill that will. Likewise, when we submit our will to His will, we become teachable, available, useful, and fruitful citizens in the Kingdom of Heaven. Being empty of self is a blessing because it allows us to be full of Jesus.

So, are you full of Jesus or are you full of yourself? Remember, what you do for God does not make you righteous. Nor does it make you more important and more powerful in His kingdom. Have you developed an attitude of self-righteousness? Ask the Lord to help you remove any thoughts of self-importance. That's when you'll begin to enjoy the blessing of emptiness.

Day 31

The Beatitudes: The Blessing of Grief

"Blessed are those who mourn, for they shall be comforted."
Matthew 5:4

One of the greatest deterrents to revival in the American church is a lack of grief over our own sin. The baseline for what the average professing Christian considers sinful has been lowered tremendously in recent years. If a behavior isn't punishable by law, then we can pretty much find a way to rationalize or excuse it.

It's important to remember that the Beatitudes build on one another. The ability to mourn over personal sin begins with being poor in spirit (Matthew 5:3). When we practice emptying ourselves of things such as self-righteousness, self-sufficiency, and self-indulgence, then we'll grieve when those sins start to raise their ugly heads. We fail to put on the righteousness of Christ when we ignore any sin.

Love makes grief possible. We do not mourn for what we do not love. Our sin grieves the heart of God because He loves us — enough that He sacrificed His Son in our place. When we see our sin in that light it brings grief; not just because of the sin itself but because we had to deny Him in order for it to exist in the first place. Only genuine love for Jesus brings conviction and grief over sin.

Too often we fail to recognize the harm sin does, causing us to forfeit the comfort found in the grace of Jesus Christ. In other words, we restrain the very thing we desperately need and what Jesus graciously desires to give: forgiveness and cleansing. The Holy Spirit comforts generously when we rightly grieve over our sin. That's when grief gives way to gladness, allowing us to know and live in the joy of our salvation.

So, how do you respond to your own sin? Resist the temptation to excuse it or ignore it. The power to overcome that sin starts by facing and confessing it. When you view your sin as God does, then it will grieve your heart. But remember, God promises the comfort of His Spirit. Yes, there is blessing in godly grieving.

Day 32

The Beatitudes: The Blessing of Gentleness

"Blessed are the gentle, for they shall inherit the earth." Matthew 5:5

The third Beatitude, gentleness, is often characterized as a personality trait; either you have it or you don't. While it's true that some people tend to be gentler in their responses than others, every believer should develop this important trait.

Gentleness is not the absence of anger but the discipline and discernment to be angry over the right things, at the right time, and with the right tone. Those who are gentle rest in the truth that vengeance and victory belong to God. Their pursuit, therefore, is the righteousness of Christ — not retaliation for being wronged.

Remember, each Beatitude builds on the next. The first two bring us to the realization that we have nothing to offer to God within ourselves; we're empty. Then comes the recognition that our sin grieves the Lord, which causes us to mourn over our sin but also invites the comfort of the Holy Spirit through the forgiveness and grace of Jesus Christ. Seeing ourselves as God sees us paves the way to respond to the faults of others with gentleness.

The life Jesus describes in the Beatitudes is not one we can live in and of ourselves. These traits are only possible in the supernatural life of Christ through the indwelling of the Holy Spirit. Do you find it difficult to respond to others in gentleness? First, ask God to reveal any prideful attitudes you may have developed. Confess those attitudes as sin, then fully submit your spirit to His Spirit.

As a result of developing the trait of gentleness, we are freed from attitudes of self-importance and from the expectation to be recognized for personal accomplishments. This way of thinking allows us to avoid the pitfalls of self-pity and the petty things of life. Gentleness offers kindness and respect without expecting anything in return. One might think that such people will be pushovers on this earth, when in fact, the gentle will inherit it.

Day 33

The Beatitudes:
The Blessing of a Righteous Appetite

"Blessed are those who hunger and thirst for righteousness, for they shall be satisfied." Matthew 5:6

Diet and exercise are critical to physical health and maturity. Can you imagine eating just one meal a week and sustaining an active and productive life? You might succeed for a week or two before your energy begins to decrease significantly. Well, our appetite is just as important when it comes to being spiritually healthy.

The hunger and thirst that Jesus speaks of in Matthew 5:6 is a believer's desire to consistently walk in fellowship with Him. It's the same hunger and thirst Jesus had for fellowship with His Father when He lived on the earth. This appetite for righteousness is the work of the Holy Spirit, who desires intimate communion with the Father. The Spirit creates the same desire in Christ's followers by revealing the truth of Scripture. This righteous hunger is also driven by exercising our faith as we walk in obedience to what we've digested.

Jesus promises that those who hunger and thirst for righteousness will be satisfied by what He offers, with no need to look for anything else. Why? Because living in the righteousness of Christ provides us with His strength, His peace, and His joy — regardless of the circumstances we face. It's the reason the apostle Paul was content regardless of having much or having nothing at all; he was satisfied and sustained by his relationship with Jesus Christ in the fullness of the Holy Spirit (Philippians 4:11).

Do you, like Paul, have a spiritual hunger for the Bread of Life and a thirst for the Living Water? Or, are you missing meals at the Lord's table? Pull up a chair, or better yet, take a knee. Once you begin to live fully in the righteousness of Christ, you will be miserable trying to find satisfaction in anything else. When you satisfy your spiritual appetite, it spills out in prayers of thanksgiving and praise to God. That's when you'll discover the blessing that comes with a righteous appetite.

Day 34

The Beatitudes: The Blessing of Mercy

"Blessed are the merciful, for they shall receive mercy." Matthew 5:7

As we continue looking at the Sermon on the Mount, it's important to recognize that the Beatitudes are not commands to obey but rather the character of Christ to display. In His righteousness, Jesus displayed mercy and forgiveness; whereas the self-righteous nature of the Scribes and Pharisees displayed condemnation and judgment. While they demanded more effort in works and better sacrifices, Jesus offered compassion. He saw people in need of rest from the burden of living under the weight of the Law.

One of the ways that Christ's followers display His righteousness is by having compassion for others. The mercy and forgiveness we receive *from* Christ compels us to share the mercy that is *in* Christ. The righteousness of Christ doesn't make us superior to people without Jesus. It makes us sensitive to their need and calls us to act in compassion.

Being merciful results in receiving mercy from God. Although this blessing is the promise in Matthew 5:7, it should not be our motivation to be merciful to others. Holy Spirit-led acts of compassion are not compelled by the reward but by the needs of hurting people. Offering mercy in the righteousness of Christ is compassion without the expectation of compensation.

Jesus is merciful to us, not because we can offer anything in return, but because He loves us. Showing mercy to others isn't repaying Jesus for bearing our sins on the Cross. Being merciful displays the righteousness of Christ to others because His nature dwells within us. We are blessed because He is glorified and others are comforted.

Are you offering the same kind of compassion to the people around you that Jesus has shown to you? Ask God to reveal where a judgmental attitude of condemnation or self-righteousness might have developed in your thinking. We know what a blessing it is to receive God's mercy, but there is also great blessing in being merciful.

Day 35

The Beatitudes: The Blessing of a Pure Heart

"Blessed are the pure in heart, for they shall see God." Matthew 5:8

Religious hypocrisy has always been a problem. Hypocrites value outward appearance more than inward purity. That's why the religious leaders in Jesus' day were so angry with Him. He exposed the sinful condition of their hearts, calling their works useless because their motive was to exalt themselves without any regard to God's glory. Having a pure heart begins with pure motives. It means you possess a sincerity of heart and a clarity of mind that's free from self-interest.

Next, a pure heart is not divided. There is no confusion regarding who is Lord and Master in your life. Jesus said that if we love Him, we'll keep His commandments; which is the natural response of a pure heart. Absolute obedience to the will of God, from the Word of God, characterizes this kind of life. If we're pure in heart, then we aren't flippant or careless about sin. Instead, sin breaks our hearts because it grieves the Holy Spirit and because we desire to be faithful and steadfast. Being pure in heart means we're willing to humble ourselves in confession and repentance when God reveals sin in our lives.

The pure in heart also see God for who He is. Do you easily recognize God in His Word and in His people? Purity of heart allows us to enjoy an intimate relationship with the Father, free from the guilt and shame of our past. It means we're sensitive to God's presence throughout the day; not only in the pleasant seasons of life, but also in suffering and sorrow. When we recognize that God is there with us, then His peace gives us strength and His promises give us hope. Consequently, knowing that eternal hands hold our lives reminds us that Earth is not our home.

This describes the heart of Christ. It was a pure heart that allowed Him to see beyond the Cross to His triumph in eternity. And, it is only with His heart that we can see beyond the troubles and trials of this world. A pure heart is available to everyone who believes, placing their trust in Jesus. What condition is your heart in today? Is it divided by unconfessed sin? Remember, there's blessing found in the obedience of a pure heart.

Day 36

The Beatitudes: The Blessing of Peacemaking

"Blessed are the peacemakers, for they shall be called sons of God."
Matthew 5:9

Satan's rebellion against God was a declaration of war. Because Adam and Eve joined that rebellion, we were all plunged into spiritual warfare, making us enemies with God. But God was not willing to concede His creation to condemnation, nor was He willing to compromise His holiness for reconciliation. His plan for peace meant providing payment for our sin by the sacrifice of His only Son.

Although Jesus knew He was entering enemy territory, He came to Earth as a peacemaker. Actually, making peace between His Father and mankind possible is the entire reason He came. The blood of Christ covers us with the righteousness of Christ, giving us the honor of being God's children and allowing us to walk in fellowship with God the Father.

As those who have accepted God's generous peace offering, we are now to be peacemakers, literally begging others to make peace with God. *"Therefore if anyone is in Christ, he is a new creature; the old things passed away; behold, new things have come. Now all these things are from God, who reconciled us to Himself through Christ and gave us the ministry of reconciliation, namely, that God was in Christ reconciling the world to Himself, not counting their trespasses against them, and He has committed to us the word of reconciliation. Therefore, we are ambassadors for Christ, as though God were making an appeal through us; we beg you on behalf of Christ, be reconciled to God"* (2 Corinthians 5:17-20).

As peacemakers, we need to realize that we will live in a war-zone as long as Satan roams the earth. Ephesians 6:14-17 describes the spiritual armor we need for the battle. We're told, *"shod your feet with the preparation of the Gospel of peace"* (v15). Simply put, we are to always be ready to share the good news of salvation through Jesus Christ. Nothing exhibits the nature of Christ more than telling others how to have peace with God.

What about you today? Are you experiencing the blessing of being a biblical peacemaker? When you slip on your shoes this week, remember to also lace up with the Gospel of peace. Let's go out and tell someone about Jesus today and discover the blessing of peacemaking!

Day 37

The Beatitudes: The Blessing of Persecution

"Blessed are those who have been persecuted for the sake of righteousness, for theirs is the kingdom of heaven. Blessed are you when people insult you and persecute you, and falsely say all kinds of evil against you because of Me. Rejoice and be glad, for your reward in heaven is great; for in the same way they persecuted the prophets who were before you."
Matthew 5:10–12

In today's passage Jesus tells us to expect hatred, trouble, and persecution if we choose to follow Him. How's that for truth in advertising? Now, Jesus isn't talking about the ordinary troubles of life. Nor does He mean the issues that arise from voicing our social and political convictions. The blessing of persecution is the result of suffering on account of Christ. We need to understand the difference between suffering for His sake and suffering for our sake.

Sometimes, followers of Christ bring unnecessary suffering upon themselves by *how* they choose to proclaim His name. Jesus does not say to be obnoxious, offensive, or inappropriately overzealous when we share our faith. Be careful. That kind of behavior is not pleasing to the Father and it's not the example of our Lord.

You see, the world does not respond with indifference to those who proclaim the name of Jesus Christ and who demonstrate His righteousness. The American mindset of suffering for Christ is somewhat skewed. We tend to forget that Christian churches in other parts of the world are under attack, literally. Believers are abducted, detained without trial, imprisoned, and even killed. Jesus says that the reward of the persecuted is the kingdom of heaven, which is why believers should possess a strong eternal mindset. *"For I consider that the sufferings of this present time are not worthy to be compared with the glory that is to be revealed to us"* (Romans 8:18).

When our lives demonstrate the righteousness of Christ, we don't have to go looking for trouble, trouble will find us! But believers will never walk into any situation that Jesus hasn't already been in or be in any circumstance where He is not present. As you go about your week, boldly speak the name of Jesus — come what may; just make sure you're also displaying His character. And remember, the blessing of persecution is the promise that this world is not our home!

Day 38

Rediscovering the Joy of Corporate Worship

"All the people went away to eat, to drink, to send portions and to celebrate a great festival, because they understood the words which had been made known to them." Nehemiah 8:12

Not too long ago it would've been hard to image a scenario in which American believers couldn't gather for corporate worship. Then came COVID-19. Week after week of virtual church raises questions about what gathering again looks like. Well, in Nehemiah 8:1-12, we see Israel rediscovering the joy of corporate worship.

The people who gathered to hear Ezra read the Law of Moses had returned to Jerusalem from 70 years of captivity in Babylon. So, for over a generation, adversity prevented them from hearing God's Word corporately. Today's church can learn three things from the response of these Jewish exiles.

First, look upward in worship (vv5-6). As Ezra opened the book, the people spontaneously responded in worship of God and in reverence for His Word. Today, many have lost their sense of awe for the things of the Lord. What used to be a day of rest and worship has become a day of leisure and laundry. Hopefully, the freedom to hear God's Word corporately is something we'll no longer take for granted.

Next, look inward in repentance (v9). As the meaning of what was being read was explained, God's instructions became clear. The reality of their sin caused genuine grief, even in the midst of this joyous occasion. Few pastors still preach repentance, which is why few people truly grieve over their sins. When the whole counsel of Scripture is proclaimed, it brings the conviction of the Holy Spirit and confession of sin.

And then, look outward in service (vv10, 12). While grieving over their sin was appropriate, this was not a time for sackcloth and ashes. As they departed, their attention was on helping those who didn't have the means to celebrate the joyous occasion. In corporate worship, we get to soak up the joy of the Lord, but we're not meant to remain full sponges. God desires to squeeze those blessings onto others through acts of love and service.

What corporate worship looks like going forward depends completely on us. Have you grown accustomed to the convenience of couch church? Or, has adversity increased your desire to worship and study God's Word together? America desperately needs to rediscover the joy of corporate worship. Revival can begin when we, as God's people, look upward in worship, inward in repentance, and outward in service.

Day 39

Rediscovering the Joy of Spiritual Community

"Then on the second day the heads of fathers' households of all the people, the priests and the Levites were gathered to Ezra the scribe that they might gain insight into the words of the law." Nehemiah 8:13

One of the ripple effects of COVID-19 is a feeling of disconnect from spiritual community. That's why taking part in a small group is more important than ever. Believers can still encourage one another, share prayer needs, and discuss Scripture. And connecting with a small group of believers prompts us to act on what we learn.

That's essentially what happened the day after revival broke out in Israel. When a group of leaders gathered to read God's Law, they rediscovered the spiritual aspect to one of their traditions. During captivity, the Feast of Tabernacles had become more of a community harvest festival than a spiritual observance. But they didn't just discuss it, they spread the word and encouraged one another to obey God's Law. As a result, all of Israel rediscovered the joy of living together in spiritual community (vv14-17).

The same is true for us today. There's simply no substitute for having a spiritual community. Our walk with the Lord is more consistent when we "do life" with a group of other believers. And like the Israelites, we help one another celebrate the full meaning of our most holy days, which have simply become seasonal holidays in our culture.

The danger these days is that we get used to watching church rather than participating. Ask yourself, "Who missed me when our church couldn't meet?" Specific names and faces come to mind more quickly by taking part in a Bible study class.

So, if you're missing out on the joy of spiritual community, then join a small group this week. Not only will your walk with the Lord be encouraged, but your presence will encourage others.

Day 40

What Does National Repentance Look Like?

"While they stood in their place, they read from the book of the law of the Lord their God for a fourth of the day; and for another fourth they confessed and worshiped the Lord their God." Nehemiah 9:3

Many Christians wonder if the pandemic will result in revival. At this point, we don't see much recognition of God's character and faithfulness, much less an overwhelming desire for His Word. So, what does national repentance look like? Well, it begins with those who claim the name of Christ exhibiting the same heart and mind we see in Nehemiah 9. We need to rediscover personal revival.

First, God's people hungered for God's Word. Their desire for God was so great that they listened for six hours, while standing! Do you have that kind of desire to understand Scripture? A hunger for God's Word is more than just reading it. We need to become students of the Bible. Otherwise, our minds drift to the world's way of thinking, which always leads to rebellion against God.

Israel also focused on the Lord. While the majority of Nehemiah 9 is a corporate prayer of confession, it begins with worship. Israel praised God's character (vv5-8) then recounted His faithfulness (vv9-15). Our nation no longer recognizes accountability to God because so few acknowledge Him as Lord and Creator. Recognizing

God's character, as well as His faithfulness in our lives, is a necessary element of revival.

The result was national repentance. Scripture reminded Israel of God's just and righteous character, and their sinfulness stood out in contrast. God's people openly confessed their personal sins and the sins of their forefathers. The path to repentance hasn't changed. When we open the Bible, seeking God Himself, we cannot help but see ourselves as He does.

So, examine your own prayers. How much time do you spend in praise and thanksgiving compared to making requests? Personal revival can start right here. Underline the names and attributes of God in Israel's prayer, then pray those things back to Him in a spirit of worship.

Next, highlight phrases that point out the Lord's faithfulness to Israel: *"You saw, You led, You gave…"* What events in your own life do these accounts bring to mind? Spend time thanking God for His faithfulness. Then circle the words, *"But they,"* indicating Israel's disobedience to the Lord. Ask Him to reveal where you've been guilty of similar things, confessing them as sin.

Scripture and prayer are as essential to national repentance today as they were in Nehemiah's time. Will you determine to develop a habit of personal time with God? Not just quickly reading a verse, but really studying Scripture, praising His character, and recounting His faithfulness.

Day 41

Genuine Spiritual Renewal

"...to walk in God's law, which was given through Moses, God's servant, and to keep and to observe all the commandments of God our Lord, and His ordinances and His statutes." Nehemiah 10:29

Nehemiah 8-10 describes the kind of spiritual renewal our nation needs today. Like these Jewish exiles, many of us have a new appreciation for living in spiritual community with other believers. And, we're rediscovering the joy of gathering for worship. But spiritual renewal is more than a feeling. It also involves commitment and obedience. Nehemiah 10 reveals three specific commitments that grow out of genuine spiritual renewal.

One of the most basic indicators of spiritual renewal is committing to a life of separation (v30). Israel's faith had been weakened by living among and marrying people who worshipped idols and false gods. Sound familiar? According to 2 Corinthians 6:14-16, we're to separate ourselves from anything not in harmony with Christ. That means building our close relationships around Him alone. As a result, we help to strengthen one another's faith.

An important aspect of separation is honoring a day of worship (v31). The Sabbath had become just another day to buy, sell, and work. So, the Israelites committed to once again reverence it as holy. Today, Sunday is the day we celebrate our risen Lord. Focusing on worship one day a week better prepares us to live for Jesus the other six days of the week.

Spiritual renewal also brings a sense of responsibility for God's house (vv32-39). The details in these verses reveal not only a commitment of their time, but of their finances as well. Far too many Christians show up to sit and soak rather than to serve. God calls each believer to some area of responsibility within the local church. We, too, can commit that *"We will not neglect the house of our God"* (v39).

How does your life back up your profession of faith in Jesus Christ? Is your faith evident by your obedience to the Lord? If we want America to have a spiritual awakening, then God's people must lead the way. So, as we step back into life as a spiritual community, let's make sure to include commitments to separation and service.

Day 42

Temptation: The Master of Deception

"But I am afraid that, as the serpent deceived Eve by his craftiness, your minds will be led astray from the simplicity and purity of devotion to Christ." 2 Corinthians 11:3

Deception is the act of leading someone to believe something that is not true. It's presenting a lie in such a way that it looks and feels like the truth. Satan has been a master of deception since the first temptation in the Garden of Eden. And we still fall for it! As with Eve, he tempts us by creating just enough doubt in our minds to draw us away from what God actually says.

Yet, Scripture tells us that it's our responsibility to not be deceived. Consider the following passages. *"And Jesus answered and said to them, "See to it that no one misleads you"* (Matthew 24:4); *"Let no one deceive you with empty words…"* (Ephesians 5:6a); *"Do not be deceived…"* (Galatians 6:7).

But we don't know what we don't know? Right? After all, if we know we're being deceived, then it's not deception. Or is it? Think of it this way. An illusionist is a master of deception. He misleads our senses to make something untrue seem true. But knowledge is power. We know that it's impossible for a person to walk through a wall. So even though it looks real, we know it's misleading.

It's the same in the spiritual realm. We're most vulnerable when we're most ignorant. We risk walking headlong into deception when we don't examine what we hear by reading God's Word for ourselves. 1 Timothy 4:1 warns, *"But the Spirit explicitly says that in later times some will fall away from the faith, paying attention to deceitful spirits and doctrines of demons."* That's why the Bible instructs us, *"Beloved, do not believe every spirit, but test the spirits to see whether they are from God, because many false prophets have gone out into the world"* (1 John 4:1).

The first step to overcoming temptation is to recognize when your mind is being misled by either worldly thinking or false doctrine. How is Satan tempting you to believe something that is not true? Remember, an increasing knowledge of God and His Word will reveal Satan's illusions for what they are — cheap tricks. Then, determine to obey what you hear from the Word of God, which makes you less vulnerable to the master of deception.

Day 43

Temptation: Tempted or Tested?

"The thief comes only to steal and kill and destroy; I came that they may have life, and have it abundantly." John 10:10

What's the difference between being tempted to sin and having our faith tested? It's an important distinction to make. John 10:10 shows us the key to determining whether we're being tempted or tested. We see two people, each with a different purpose. The thief brings death and destruction, while Jesus gives abundant life.

The person behind every temptation is the thief — the devil. He is a liar, a destroyer, and our enemy. That tells us a lot about the purpose of temptation, doesn't it? Satan desires to keep lost people in bondage to sin and to stop believers from experiencing a victorious Christian life. When he influences us to act independently *of* God we become ineffective *for* God. Once we step outside of God's will, he knows we're vulnerable to all kinds of attacks and discouragement.

On the other hand, God never uses temptation to test His people. James 1:13 tells us, *"for God cannot be tempted by evil, nor does He Himself tempt anyone."* Just as temptation is rooted in Satan's attributes, the testing of our faith is based on the character of God. When the Lord allows a situation to test your faith, it's for your good — always. The Bible describes several purposes for God's testing:

- Proves the authenticity of faith (Genesis 22:15-18)
- Removes impurity (Job 23:10)
- Increases spiritual fruit (John 15:2)
- Produces spiritual endurance and maturity (James 1:3-4)
- Results in praise, glory, and honor to Jesus Christ (1 Peter 1:7)

Once you recognize the difference, it's striking. Satan wants us to live in fear and spiritual poverty, while Jesus saved us to live in the abundance of His joy, peace, strength, and wisdom.

So, are you being tempted or tested? Understanding which it is determines your response. Does the situation require you to act against God's character or His Word? Then it's a temptation from the enemy, who wants to destroy you. Flee from it. Does the situation require you to depend upon the Holy Spirit for direction and strength? Then embracing the challenge will grow your faith and strengthen your character. Remember, your dependence on Jesus is your independence from sin's persuasion, power, and purpose.

Day 44

Temptation: The Pain of Presumptuous Sin

"Also keep back Your servant from presumptuous sins; let them not rule over me; then I will be blameless, and I shall be acquitted of great transgression." Psalm 19:13

As we've been talking about temptation, we've seen how Satan uses deception as a tool to tempt believers. One of the most effective ways he does this is to present the thought that we can willfully choose to sin and it will somehow be okay — like jumping off a cliff without suffering the consequences. When a believer knows a certain thought or action is sinful and chooses to do it anyway, that's presumptuous sin.

In Psalm 19, we see David's desire to be ruled by the Lord, not by his own flesh. He recognized that deliberately choosing to sin put him at particular risk. And no one understood the pain of presumptuous sin more than David. His prayer in Psalm 51 describes a broken man, consumed with guilt and desperate for God's forgiveness. It's the same for us. Presumptuous sin steals our joy and wrecks our walk with Christ.

Remember, a born-again believer has a new nature — the nature of Christ. So, we're not under the rule of sin because the death and resurrection of Jesus broke its power. Unfortunately, we still live in a body with our sinful nature. Satan will use that old nature to temp us. Even though our flesh wars against the righteousness of Christ that dwells within us, we don't have to sin. Romans 6:14 tells us, *"For sin shall not be master over you, for you are not under law but under grace."* By choosing to sin, we're presuming upon God's grace. Do you see how deceptive that is? Satan dangles the very grace of God like a get out of jail free card.

When you think about it, sinning by choice requires a certain amount of arrogance. We either think we know enough about God and Scripture to control the consequences, or we plan to ask God's forgiveness after the fact. That's a dangerous way for a believer to live.

David ends Psalm 19 by saying, *"Let the words of my mouth and the meditation of my heart be acceptable in Your sight, O Lord, my rock and my Redeemer"* (Psalm 19:14). Is that your prayer today? The only way to be free from the pain of presumptuous sin is to completely surrender to the Lord; to desire to please Him with everything we think, say, and do.

Day 45

Temptation: Victory Over Temptation

"For we do not have a high priest who cannot sympathize with our weakness, but one who has been tempted in all things as we are, yet without sin." Hebrews 4:15

The temptation to sin is inevitable. No one is exempt, including Jesus. His victory over temptation means that we can also be victorious. So, how does understanding His victory over temptation help us?

First, don't confuse being tempted with being sinful. Jesus was tempted. So, the temptation itself is not a sin. What you do with the sinful thoughts and attitudes that cross your mind determines whether or not you actually sin. In order to have victory over temptation, we must continually *"take every thought captive to the obedience of Christ"* (2 Corinthians 10:5).

Next, realize that our humanity is not a valid excuse to sin. We sometimes forget that Jesus was fully human when He lived on the earth (Hebrews 2:14, 17). Although He lived in a world ruled by sin, He never had a sinful thought or committed a sinful deed. Hebrews 2:18 tells us, *"For since He Himself was tempted...He is able to come to the aid of those who are tempted."* Our victory over temptation comes by accepting His help rather than making excuses.

Finally, we have the same advantages for victory over temptation as Jesus: the Holy Spirit and the Word of God. Although the Holy Spirit indwells every believer, we have to submit to His promptings in order to operate in His power. Still, that doesn't mean He'll always guide you on paths that avoid temptation. Matthew 4:1 tells us that Jesus was led by the Spirit into the wilderness to be tempted by the devil. When you surrender to the control of the Holy Spirit, as Jesus did, God will give you victory over whatever temptation you face. The Bible also says that Jesus responded to temptation with Scripture. While the world around us denies the truth and authority of God's Word, Satan does not. He knows full well that he cannot stand against it.

Yes, Adam and Eve lost the battle over temptation, but Jesus won the war! Because He experienced every temptation we face and overcame, we are free from sin's penalty and power. Jesus acts as our eternal high priest, not to condemn us when we're tempted, but to help us. When we live in dependence upon the Holy Spirit and under the authority of God's Word, the victory of salvation is also our victory over temptation.

Day 46

Temptation: The Guilt-Free Life

"Therefore, there is now no condemnation for those who are in Christ Jesus. For the law of the Spirit of life in Christ Jesus has set you free from the law of sin and of death." Romans 8:1-2

Far too many believers live in the bondage of guilt, allowing their feelings to control their faith. Constantly battling guilt is usually a failure to believe what the Bible says about who we are in Christ. We get so wrapped up in trying to *do* Christianity that we miss the joy and freedom of the guilt-free life intended for followers of Jesus.

Romans 8:1 doesn't say "there is no sin." At times, Christians sin and experience various types of spiritual failure. While God may allow us to suffer the consequences of our sins, we don't have to fear condemnation. You see, God doesn't use guilt to handle sin in the life of a believer; He uses grace. That doesn't mean He ignores sin. The Lord graciously makes us aware of it through the conviction of the Holy Spirit so we can confess it and repent from it.

Still, the enemy tries to bring that sin up again and again in our minds in order to manipulate our thinking. But the only way guilt can manipulate you, as a believer, is when you allow it to, by ignoring who you are in Christ. Look at the facts. Jesus took the wrath of our sin upon Himself on the Cross. So, placing our trust in the person and work of Jesus sets us free from God's wrath and condemnation.

Basically, we settled out of court. We are free from the penalty and power of sin for all eternity.

Just realize that your eternity has already begun. You can live the abundant life of Christ right now. Why let guilt manipulate you when Jesus has set you free? When the Holy Spirit reveals sin in your life, use 1 John 1:9 like a bar of soap, *"If we confess our sins, He is faithful and righteous to forgive us our sins and to cleanse us from all unrighteousness."* Then move on and live guilt-free in the fullness of Christ Jesus. This week, remember that the guilt-free life is Christ-filled and grace-fueled.

Day 47

The Greatest Commandment: Are You Listening?

"Hear, O Israel! The Lord our God is one Lord;" Mark 12:29b

What's the most important thing God wants us to do? That's the question posed to Jesus in Mark 12. Without hesitation, Jesus zeroed in on Deuteronomy 6:4-5. While the heart of the Greatest Commandment is about loving God, let's not skip over the Lord's instructions to listen to what He's about to say. Listening is obviously important. Jesus repeats, *"He who has ears to hear, let him hear"* fifteen times in the New Testament. So, are you listening?

There's a lot of noise in the world competing for our attention. Most of it is just clamor, promising us some kind of fulfillment or satisfaction. If we truly desire to follow Christ, then we have to choose to listen to the voice of the Holy Spirit. Despite what any other voice says, Jesus Christ is the only one who can provide what our hearts, souls, minds, and bodies crave.

That's why the next part of the command tells us, *"The Lord our God is one Lord."* Of all the world religions, the God of the Bible is unique. He alone is Lord over creation and He alone desires to have a relationship with us based on mutual love. Do your current circumstances cause you to doubt that God is paying attention or that

He loves you? The Bible says that God knows the number of hairs on your head and every tear you shed. He is very aware of your situation. The question is, are you aware of His presence in the midst of your circumstances? Are you listening for His voice?

God speaks to us primarily through Scripture. While biblical preaching and teaching are extremely important, be careful not to neglect spending time alone reading God's Word. The Holy Spirit will teach you deep truths and guide you into God's will. The Lord also speaks through our circumstances and through the Holy Spirit, but He never contradicts the Bible, which is how we know it's God speaking.

Listening and loving are two sides of the same coin. If we're going to love God with all that we are and love others as we love ourselves, then we've got to pay attention to what the One true God says. He can be heard by anyone listening for Him to speak. Are you listening today?

Day 48

The Greatest Commandment: Do You Really Love God?

"And you shall love the Lord your God...." Mark 12:30a

The word, "love" has lost its significance in our culture because we use it to describe our feelings for anyone or anything we like. Saying that we love chocolate or football diminishes our understanding of the Greatest Commandment to love God. Because our concept of love is so skewed, it's hard to answer the question, "Do you really love God?" What we need is a better understanding of biblical love.

The kind of love Jesus is talking about is the love He has for His Father and His Father has for Him. It's also the same love He has for us. You may be thinking, "How can I possibly love God the way He loves Jesus?" First, God gives us the capacity to genuinely love Him when we are saved, *"the love of God has been poured out within our hearts through the Holy Spirit who was given to us"* (Romans 5:5). Our ability to love God is simply a matter of returning the love He gives to us. This supernatural love is a gift of God's grace. We then express that love back to God through obedience to His Word.

Think of it this way: we can't physically see love, but we can see its effects. God's love for the world is seen on the Cross. In the same way, who or what we love motivates our behavior. So, our love for God can be measured by our actions. Jesus is saying that loving Him is the most important element in an obedient Christian life. At first, this command may seem self-serving on God's part. Keep in mind, though, that no one knows us better or loves us more than our Creator. His commands are for our good and for His glory.

We talk about accepting the love of God by faith, but sometimes forget that demonstrating our love for God is also a matter of faith. Not faith that we can do anything, but faith that Jesus Christ, Himself, can love through us. As born-again believers, we are forgiven through the blood of Jesus and given the life of Jesus, so that we can live and love in the power of Jesus. Have you personally recognized and accepted God's love for you? If so, then demonstrate today that you really love God by being obedient to His Word.

Day 49

The Greatest Commandment: How Much Do You Love God?

"And you shall love the Lord your God with all your heart, and with all your soul, and with all your mind, and with all your strength." Mark 12:30

Many Christians have a linear idea of what loving God looks like. We come up with formulas such as, God first, family second, work/school third, etc. While these priorities are good, we need to go further than just loving God first. Let's consider the question, "How *much* do you love God?"

You see, linear thinking limits our love for God in two ways. First, it makes our relationship with Christ seem like a "to do" list. We may think that doing more for God than for anyone else means we must love Him enough. But the Greatest Commandment isn't about our works. Secondly, linear thinking limits our love for God because it compartmentalizes our lives into categories: God, family, work, school, church, and community. Love for God should be expressed through everyday life, like how we relate to our families and how we perform our job or schoolwork.

So, what does the Greatest Commandment actually tell us to do? Well, we are to love the Lord with every aspect of our being. Loving God with all of your heart means submitting your emotions to God. Loving God with all of your soul means surrendering your will to God. Loving God with all of your mind means centering your thoughts on

God. And loving God with all of your strength means presenting your body in service to God.

When we love God with everything we have, then He expresses His life in everything we feel, think, desire, and do. This type of love moves our relationship with Christ from being an item on a list or in a compartment, to being the whole of our identity. Rather than being linear, it's all-encompassing.

What about you today? How much do you love God? The Greatest Commandment exposes your greatest need, because without Jesus you can't possibly meet this standard of love. It requires living in the fullness of the indwelling Holy Spirit. If you'll surrender to His love, then life will change from a list of things you have to do, to a life of love that you want to live. Remember, all means all!

Day 50

The Greatest Commandment: Do You Love Like Jesus?

"The second is this, 'You shall love your neighbor as yourself.'" Mark 12:31

According to Jesus, the Greatest Commandment is loving God with all of our heart, soul, mind, and strength. But He doesn't stop there. The second greatest commandment should be an outcome of the first. When we love God with our entire being it naturally creates an awareness of the people around us. Jesus is the perfect example of living in all-out love for God and in loving service to others. So, do you love like Jesus?

First, let's consider how Jesus responded to the young lawyer who asked, *"And who is my neighbor?"* (Luke 10:29). Rather than giving a list, Jesus told the parable of the Good Samaritan. You see, the Jewish rabbis redefined "neighbor" to mean only other Jews. Jesus broadened the scope of their thinking to include people who didn't look like them or live like them. It was the Samaritan, not the priest or the Levite, who demonstrated Christ-like love.

Likewise, our neighbors are not limited to the people who live next door or who go to church with us. It even goes beyond the lost people at work and at school. Our neighbors are also the strangers we pass at the shopping center and in grocery store. Loving like Jesus means we seek to benefit those people, even at our own expense.

If we're honest, most Christians don't even love other believers the way God says we should. We're told in 1 John 4:20, *"If someone says, 'I love God,' and hates his brother, he is a liar; for the one who does not love his brother whom he has seen, cannot love God whom he has not seen."* Now, we may not come out and say that we hate another follower of Christ, but the negative relationships in many churches strongly suggests that it's there, just the same.

By connecting these two commandments, Jesus urges His followers to be extensions of God's heart and God's hands. When we obediently love the Lord with all that we are, we also love other people unselfishly. The more we love God, the better we see, love, and serve others. If you find yourself trying to muster up love for other people, then you're not loving like Jesus loves. He will give you the opportunity to share His love today. Will you take it?

Day 51

Cleaning Out Your Temple

"And Jesus entered the temple and drove out all those who were buying and selling in the temple, and overturned the tables of the money changers and the seats of those who were selling doves. And He said to them, 'It is written, "My house shall be called a house of prayer;" but you are making it a robbers' den.'" Matthew 21:12-13

The week before His death on the Cross, Jesus entered the temple and described a group of people He found there as robbers and thieves. These money changers were overcharging people for animals needed for the temple sacrifices. Angered by the fact that the priests allowed this extortion and used their position as a means of profit, Jesus threw the crooks out of the temple.

But what does that have to do with believers today? There's an important personal application in 1 Corinthians 6:19-20, *"Or do you not know that your body is a temple of the Holy Spirit who is in you, whom you have from God, and that you are not your own? For you have been bought with a price: therefore glorify God in your body."*

Salvation isn't just about the pardon of sins, it's also about the purchase of the sinner. His blood paid the price for sin. If you've chosen to apply that payment to your life, then Jesus bought you. He is the owner of your spirit, your soul, and your body. Your body is a walking and breathing temple of the Holy Spirit.

If the Holy Spirit now occupies your being, what happened to the old occupant — your fleshly, sinful nature? It was crucified with Christ (Romans 6:10-11; Galatians 6:20). You didn't simply come under new management, your old nature was executed! And the Holy Spirit will not tolerate sin in His temple. As a believer in Christ, you no longer have the right to say, "It's my body and my life."

What is the state of your temple today? Is it in need of a good cleaning out? Matthew 21 vividly describes how our sin grieves the heart of God. When you're in close personal fellowship with Christ, His Spirit will convict you of anything displeasing that starts to set up shop in His temple. Don't ignore the promptings of the Holy Spirit. Choose to glorify God with your body — today and every day.

Day 52

Running Off Robbers

"And He said to them, 'It is written, "My house shall be called a house of prayer"; but you are making it a robbers' den.'" Matthew 21:13

You wouldn't dream of welcoming thieves into your home. You might even take precautions to protect your family and your belongings from those who would rob what is rightfully yours. Too often, though, we throw open the door to spiritual robbers. Sinful attitudes and habits rob us of the joy of our salvation, the strength of the Lord, and the peace that passes all understanding. As a result, we become double-minded and live in the defeat of doubt and despair.

Our bodies are under God's ownership as the temple of the Holy Spirit. When we live as such, He begins to remove things that are in conflict with the desired purposes of God. If, however, we choose to rebel against the ownership of Christ, then spiritual robbers can actually become rulers in our lives. We give the Holy Spirit permission to run these robbers off by willful submission to God.

How do you run thieves and robbers off? Jesus used Scripture when He cleansed the temple. We also know that robbers are liars, and liars hate the truth. In John 17:17 Jesus prayed, *"Sanctify them in the truth; Your word is truth."* The world is full of lies that can keep us from enjoying healthy fellowship with Jesus Christ. The truth of God's Word can defeat any lie thrown at us by the enemy.

God desires that each believer be a house of prayer; that we keep a clear channel of communication with Him, which is critical when battling the enemy. But also know this, *"If I regard wickedness in my heart the Lord will not hear"* (Psalm 66:18). The more of God's Word we know and believe, the better we are at dealing with the lies of this world.

What's currently robbing your joy, strength, or peace? Maybe it's time to put precautions in place to protect your heart and mind from spiritual robbers. Start by flooding your mind with the truth of God's Word. Then clear up those channels of communication by confessing any sin the Holy Spirit reveals to you. Finally, submit your entire being to God's ownership and allow His Spirit to stand guard over the door to your heart and mind.

Day 53

A Grave Miscalculation

"Not everyone who says to Me, 'Lord, Lord,' will enter the kingdom of heaven, but he who does the will of My Father who is in heaven will enter. Many will say to Me on that day, 'Lord, Lord, did we not prophesy in Your name, and in Your name cast out demons, and in Your name perform many miracles?'" Matthew 7:21–22

Many people who claim the name of Christ will not go to Heaven. They may have walked down an aisle, repeated the words of a prayer, and joined a church. They may even have done good deeds in His name. In spite of all this, Jesus will say to them, *"Depart from me"* (v23). Let's look at a few possible reasons many will make such a grave miscalculation.

First, many are counting on their own actions to get them into Heaven. This way of thinking puts the cart before the horse. Ephesians 2:8-10 explains that good works are a result of salvation, not the cause. Any action, in and of itself, cannot qualify us for Heaven.

Many are also seeking the security of Heaven without any ramifications in the here and now. They view salvation as nothing more than a fire insurance plan. In other words, they don't really want a relationship with Jesus Christ, they just don't want to go to Hell. Real, saving grace salvation is more than Jesus getting us out of Hell. It's also about Jesus getting into us.

Ephesians 2 goes on to say that before salvation we were, *"separate from Christ...strangers to the covenants of promise, having no hope and without God in the world. But now in Christ Jesus you who formerly were far off have been brought near by the blood of Christ"* (vv12-13). This close, personal relationship means we live in anticipation of Heaven because Jesus is there.

If you call yourself a Christian, then it's good to examine what your salvation is based upon. Are you counting on what you've done to get you into Heaven or on what Jesus did on the Cross? Did you repeat the words of a prayer just in case Hell turns out to be real?

If you've made a grave miscalculation, then today can be your day of salvation. Don't live a minute longer in fear of Hell. Jesus is waiting for you to place your complete faith and trust in Him. As a believer, obedience to His Word becomes something you desire to do out of sheer love and loyalty to Christ. Authentic Christianity lives each day in His power and for His purpose.

Day 54

No Regrets

"For I am already being poured out as a drink offering, and the time of my departure has come. I have fought the good fight, I have finished the course, I have kept the faith." 2 Timothy 4:6-7

Sitting in a Roman prison awaiting his execution, the apostle Paul had great insight on living with no regrets. He had spent the last 30 years preaching the Gospel of Jesus Christ all over Europe and into Asia Minor. Think about what Paul had endured in those years: numerous beatings, including three times with rods; 39 lashes with a whip on five occasions; stoned once; and three shipwrecks! Additionally, he described, *"the daily pressure on me of concern for all the churches"* (2 Corinthians 11:28).

Given Paul's present circumstances, you might think he felt self-pity or even questioned God's faithfulness. Yet, instead of regretting the pain Paul anticipated the future reward ceremony in Heaven. In today's passage he gives an example of how we, too, can live a life without regrets.

First, view your life as an offering given, not a toll taken. This change in attitude makes every day an act of worship. Next, fight the right fights. Go to battle over the eternal, not the petty drama of everyday life. Then, stay focused on eternity rather than dwelling on the past or getting distracted in the present.

Finally, remain faithful to the end. Persevering faith is the result of passion for Jesus Christ. We emulate Paul's faith by treating every day as an opportunity to glorify Christ through seeking the lost and strengthening the Church.

Paul didn't see his death as an execution but as an extraction, *"The Lord will rescue me from every evil deed, and will bring me safely to His heavenly kingdom; to Him be the glory forever and ever. Amen"* (2 Timothy 4:18). Paul wasn't leaving home; he was going home — without any regrets.

Day 55

The Value of One

"I tell you that in the same way, there will be more joy in heaven over one sinner who repents than over ninety-nine righteous persons who need no repentance." Luke 15:7

One day an old man was walking along the beach. It was low tide and the sand was littered with thousands of stranded starfish that the water had carried in and then left behind. The man began walking very carefully so as not to step on any of the beautiful creatures. Since the animals still seemed to be alive, he considered picking some of them up and putting them back in the water. He knew they would die if left on the dry sand but he reasoned that he could not possibly help them all, so he chose to do nothing and continued walking.

Soon afterward, the man came upon a child on the beach who was frantically throwing one starfish after another back into the sea. The man stopped and asked, "What are you doing?" "I'm saving the starfish," the child replied. "Why waste your time? There are so many you can't save them all so what does it matter?" argued the man. Without hesitation, the child picked up another starfish and tossed the starfish back into the water. "It matters to this one," the child explained.

In a culture that stereotypes people by groups, we often lose the value of individuals. Scripture teaches us that God values the life of one person just as much as He values the life of all. When Jesus was on the earth, He took time to serve individuals with the same compassion that He served the many. His earthly mission was to seek and to save the lost. So, yes, He preached salvation to the multitudes but He also sought out individuals such as Zacchaeus and the Samaritan woman at the well.

We can be easily overwhelmed by all that's happening in the world around us. The needs are so enormous and evil so prevalent, that many Christians want to pull up the draw bridge and isolate themselves. That's not what Jesus did. We need to see the value of serving one person the way we desire to serve many. Look for the individuals God puts in your path. Will you take the opportunity to tell one person about Jesus today? Heaven will rejoice when you do.

Day 56

Knowing God's Will: Presentation

"Therefore I urge you, brethren, by the mercies of God, to present yours bodies a living and holy sacrifice, acceptable to God, which is your spiritual service of worship." Romans 12:1

If you are a Bible-believing, church-going follower of Christ, then you probably have a desire to know God's will. You might even aspire to live obediently *in* His will. The average Christian, however, treats God's will like some kind of Easter egg hunt. They act as if God's will is hidden; leaving us to search endlessly in hopes of happening upon it. We need to change our thinking.

At the end of Romans 12:2 the apostle Paul writes, *"so that you may prove what the will of God is, that which is good and acceptable and perfect."* Since God wants us to know His will, we need to back up to Romans 12:1 and find out how to get there. It begins with a presentation, *"present your bodies a living and holy sacrifice."*

Paul challenges us to absolute surrender in view of the incredible mercy God showed in the sacrifice of His only Son on the Cross. Paul isn't suggesting that we have to do something in order to gain God's mercy; he is asking us to respond to the grace and mercy already given.

Although Paul is not demanding, he strongly urges us to do something very important: present ourselves. You see, in order to know God's will we have to deliberately, intentionally, and completely place ourselves at God's disposal. We achieve this by considering ourselves, *"dead to sin, but alive to God in Christ Jesus"* (Romans 6:11).

Knowing God's will is about who we're filled with rather than what we're trying to find. We live the sacrificial Christian life when we trust God to do His will *through* us. Someone once said, "To present yourself as a living sacrifice is to sign a blank check and let God fill in the amount." Do you want to know God's will? Then empty yourself of your own will. Present yourself to God as an act of worship to be used completely at His disposal. While you may think it sounds restrictive, you'll soon discover the freedom found in spiritual transformation.

Day 57

Knowing God's Will: Contemplation

"Therefore be careful how you walk, not as unwise men but as wise, making the most of your time, because the days are evil. So then do not be foolish, but understand what the will of the Lord is. And do not get drunk with wine, for that is dissipation, but be filled with the Spirit." Ephesians 5:15-18

Volumes have been written on how to know the will of God, but have you contemplated why it's so important? God's will has a lot to do with knowing God. Too often, we treat God's will more like a mystery to solve rather than a Master to serve.

He is a rewarder of those who seek Him. Believers have a standing invitation to, *"draw near with confidence to the throne of grace, so that we can receive mercy and find grace to help in time of need"* (Hebrews 4:16). God desires to give us two things we desperately need: mercy and grace. Does that sound like someone who is trying to keep us in the dark? He knows that we need mercy and grace in abundance in order to live according to His will.

Ephesians 5:15–18 says that not knowing God's will leads to a careless, foolish, and wasteful life. Eugene Peterson helps us understand God's perspective on that kind of living. Listen to how he phrases 1 Corinthians 1:25–28 in *The Message*. "Human wisdom is so tiny, so impotent, next to the seeming absurdity of God. Human strength can't begin to compete with God's 'weakness.' Take a good look, friends, at who you were when you got called into this life. I don't see many of 'the brightest and the best' among you, not many influential, not many from high-society families. Isn't it obvious that God deliberately chose men and women that the culture overlooks and exploits and abuses, chose these 'nobodies' to expose the hollow pretensions of the 'somebodies'?"

Do you desire to understand God's will, to daily receive His gifts of mercy and grace, and to be counted among the wise? Then seek to know Him. His will is revealed in His presence as you draw near to Him. Remember, God's will is not determined by the world's definition of success. The closer you abide with Him, the more you'll gain His perspective.

Day 58

Knowing God's Will: Transformation

"And do not be conformed to this world, but be transformed by the renewing of your mind, so that you may prove what the will of God is, that which is good and acceptable and perfect." Romans 12:2

Knowing the will of God requires that we have the mind of Christ rather than the mind of the world. This involves renewal, which brings transformation. When believers think and live like the world, their faith has little to no influence on their outward behavior. However, when a believer is transformed by renewed thinking — having the mind of Christ — then inward belief determines outward behavior.

How do we renew our minds? Through God's Word. The will of God will never contradict the Word of God. That's why the Psalmist wrote, *"Your word have I treasured in my heart, that I might not sin against you"* (Psalm 119:11) and, *"Your word is a lamp unto my feet and a light to my path"* (Psalm 119:105).

Too often though, Christians rely on emotions as the best indicator for knowing the God's will; failing to engage their minds. Be careful — emotions are fickle. They will swing to and fro with your circumstances, convincing you that God's will is one thing today then quickly changing tomorrow. The mind of Christ is the same — yesterday, today, and forever.

Since knowing God's will requires a renewed mind, then it is incredibly important to pay attention to what we watch and to be discerning about what we listen to. Remember, what you allow to entertain you can also entrap you. Do you want to know the will of God? Then carefully evaluate who and what you've allowed to influence your thinking.

In what area of life have you conformed to influences outside of God's Word? Are your emotions or your entertainment choices in conflict with the mind of Christ? Then determine to take, *"every thought captive to the obedience of Christ"* (2 Corinthians 10:5). A transformed mind is living proof that God's will can be known because it will be shown in and through you.

Day 59

Living in Victory: Defining Victory

"I have been crucified with Christ; and it is no longer I who live, but Christ lives in me; and the life which I now live in the flesh I live by faith in the Son of God, who loved me and gave Himself up for me." Galatians 2:20

Many believers are living depleted and defeated lives. They aren't experiencing the abundant, liberated, and victorious life promised in Scripture. Let's get really personal and change the pronoun from "they" to "us". What keeps us from living in the victory of Jesus Christ each and every day? In order to answer that question, we need to define exactly what living in victory means.

Christ gives us victory over sin, self, and Satan. So, the victorious Christian life is freedom from the penalty and power of sin. Too many believers are content with victory over the penalty of sin and stop short of claiming victory over its power in their lives. Have you tried to overcome a particular sin on your own, only to fall flat time-after-time? Well, God wouldn't tell us that something is possible without also providing the means for it. The victorious life is possible because it's Jesus living His life in us.

As we define what it means to live in victory, there are some frequent misunderstandings to clear up regarding what the victorious Christian life is not. It is not a life in which it is impossible to sin, but a life in which victory over sin is possible.

Nor is it for just a few selected "super saints." Victory over sin is His provision for every believer.

A victorious Christian life is not the absence of trouble, but the presence of God's peace and power in the midst of even the greatest difficulties. It's not life without temptation, but a life where temptation is overcome. And it's not just about outward actions and behaviors, but also victory over thoughts and attitudes.

So how about you? Would you describe your daily life as depleted, or powerful? Defeated, or victorious? Jesus has already won the victory, enabling you to live in that victory by yielding to the Holy Spirit each moment of each day. Remember, you live in victory as you live *in* Jesus.

Day 60

Living in Victory: Making the Impossible, Possible

"For as many as are the promises of God, in Him they are yes; therefore also through Him is our Amen to the glory of God through us." 2 Corinthians 1:20

Is it really God's will that we live in victory? Do we have all we need to live such a life? If the answer is yes (and it is), then being satisfied with anything less than God's will is sin. His will is for every believer to live in Him. Said another way…Jesus Christ lives His life through us. Does that sound impossible in your current situation? Well, Jesus makes the impossible life, possible.

Now, we're not talking about victory one day, "in the sweet by and by." God intends for us to live victoriously in the present tense…right now, today. We're also not talking about always gaining victory *over* our challenging circumstances. Yes, it's glorious when God removes difficulty, but the sweetest times with the Lord are often when He gives us victory *in* our circumstances.

We tend to separate spiritual ideals from everyday practical living. Although there are times we each fail to trust the Lord fully, those moments should be the exception — not the rule. We know from Scripture that it is not God's will for His children to live defeated lives. The very people who have been cleansed by the blood of Jesus and who have trusted Him for the salvation of our souls should not also be held hostage by our circumstances or emotions.

Today's passage makes it abundantly clear that all of God's promises for a victorious life are made good in the person and life of Jesus. Did you catch the phrase, *"through Him is our Amen"*? The word, "Amen" can be restated, "so be it." What seems impossible to us is possible with God simply because He has said that it is so!

In order to succeed in the victorious life, however, we must surrender to His life. What situation seems impossible to you right now? Take it to the Lord in prayer. While He has the power to remove the difficulty, He may choose to leave it in place so you learn full reliance on Him. Either way, you can live victoriously today in the person of Jesus Christ. As the embodiment of all God's promises; He makes the impossible, possible.

Day 61

Living in Victory: The Secret to Victory

"...fixing our eyes on Jesus, the author and perfecter of faith..."
Hebrews 12:2

God wants us to enjoy all that He has generously provided in His Son, Jesus. So why aren't more of us living in the victory of Christ? It's almost like the key to the victorious Christian life is a secret. However, God would not tell us to walk in victory and then hide how to do it. The secret is, there is no secret. But there are a few keys to the victorious life that we need to know.

Victory is a gift. *"But thanks be to God, who gives us the victory through our Lord Jesus Christ"* (1 Corinthians 15:57). Why do we waste time and energy trying to earn what can only be received by trusting the Lord? We couldn't afford the life of victory that God so generously gives us in His Son Jesus.

Victory begins with grace. *"For by grace you have been saved through faith; and that not of yourselves, it is the gift of God"* (Ephesians 2:8). Every Christian who experiences the victorious life has done so in the knowledge that it cannot be gained in their own strength; no matter how mentally, physically, or financially gifted they are. We are completely incapable of enjoying the victorious and abundant life without trusting, resting, and relying on the grace given us in and through the life of Jesus.

Victory is a choice. *"For you died, and your life is now hidden with Christ in God" (Colossians 3:3)*. *"...I die daily" (1 Corinthians 15:31)*. This is a deliberate choice; a conscious act of the will to surrender our minds and bodies to the will of God. It is a daily choice to die to self and live for Christ.

Living the victorious Christian life isn't modeled very often, but it's certainly not a secret. As a matter of fact, all that we've discussed about it can be wrapped up in one sentence: Let us *"fix our eyes on Jesus, the author and perfecter of faith..."* (Hebrews 12:2). Will you fix your thoughts on Him today in order to live victoriously? He is the only One Who can give us the victory!

Day 62

To Know Wisdom: Use Good Judgment

"To give prudence to the naive, to the youth knowledge and discretion"
Proverbs 1:4

Wisdom and good judgment are in short supply today. Not only does foolish behavior thrive in our culture; it's often celebrated. No book in the Bible talks more about wisdom and foolishness than Proverbs; the stated purpose of which is, *"To know wisdom..."* (1:2a). In the first seven verses, Solomon eloquently describes why his collection of wise sayings is useful. Acquiring wisdom bares itself out in one's attitudes and actions. It shows us how to use good judgment.

How do we know if we're exercising good judgment? Well, sometimes it's just applying old fashion common sense. Proverbs 14:15 tells us, *"The naive believes everything, but the sensible man considers his steps."* While the simple-minded go through life uncautious and unaware, those with good judgment give forethought to their actions. In other words, they use discretion.

Solomon urges, *"My son, let them not vanish from your sight; keep sound wisdom and discretion,"* (3:21). This careful approach to life guards against evil, perversity, deviousness, and immorality (2:11-16). And it's usually accompanied by other signs of good judgment such as knowledge and prudence (5:2, 8:12).

Now, we don't use the word prudence much these days, but a closer look adds to our understanding of good judgment. The prudent avoid places where evil is on display (22:3, 27:12); they don't lash out in anger (12:16); and they know when to be quiet (12:23, 17:28).

Does your life show evidence of good judgment? Or, do you speak impulsively and act in a reckless manner? In today's world, using common sense might make you stand out. As a matter of fact, following Christ often means not following conventional wisdom. If we want *"to know wisdom,"* then we need to embrace the teachings and sayings of wise. Exercising good judgment will not only affect your attitudes and actions; it will guard you from the foolishness of the world.

Day 63

To Know Wisdom: Listen and Learn

"A wise man will hear and increase in learning, and a man of understanding will acquire wise counsel," Proverbs 1:5

Wisdom is often associated with old age. However, one doesn't have to be old to be wise. Nor does one have to be young to be foolish. In Solomon's introduction to Proverbs, he describes the wise as those who listen and learn. Wise people become even wiser by listening to the sayings in Proverbs and by learning from their guidance (1:5).

Proverbs is pretty clear in its connection between wisdom and listening. A wise person listens to advice and instruction (8:33, 9:8-9, 10:8, 12:15, 19:20); as well as to correction and rebuke (13:1, 15:31, 19:25). The key, however, is to learn from what is said. Walking in wisdom is a process of life-long learning.

Today's verse also says we can *"acquire wise counsel"* by reading the book of Proverbs with understanding. Again, Proverbs clearly connects wisdom with seeking counsel (11:14, 13:10, 15:22). So, when it comes to listening to advice and instruction, Proverbs guides the wise to associate with other wise people. Proverbs 13:20 says, "He who walks with wise men will be wise, but the companion of fools will suffer harm."

Listening to and learning from the foolish is a road to heartache. That's why it's vital to practice discernment in our relationships. You see, godly wisdom is always hungry for godly truth and looks to acquire it from godly sources. Since God's Word is the most reliable source for wisdom, we should build friendships with people who read and apply it. This requires awareness. Wise people don't have to tell anyone they are wise. It's on display in the choices they make and the words they speak.

So, do the people in your life encourage building your faith or compromising it? Do you have at least one godly friendship where biblical wisdom and correction can be offered, as well as received? Living in wisdom is the result of understanding and applying biblical truth. Jesus often closed His teachings by saying, *"He who has ears, let them hear."* Are your ears tuned to God's sources of truth? If you want to know and walk in wisdom, then you must be willing to listen and learn.

Day 64

To Know Wisdom: Fear of the Lord

"The fear of the LORD is the beginning of knowledge," Proverbs 1:7a

No phrase in Scripture is more misunderstood than, *"fear of the Lord."* Living in fear of the Lord is very different than being afraid of Him. The phrase appears more in Proverbs than all the other books of the Bible combined. Solomon, the wisest man who ever lived, tells us that *"fear of the Lord"* is foundational to true knowledge and wisdom (9:10).

Theologians agree that *"fear of the Lord"* is synonymous with reverence for God and His Word. Such reverence creates a longing to know God more and to seek His direction. A growing knowledge of God's character fills us with awe for Who He is and generates gratitude for what He has done on our behalf. His overwhelming love for us produces a genuine desire to please to God because we love Him; not because we fear His punishment.

Seeking to know God through His Word goes far beyond just gathering facts about Him. Scripture promises the enlightenment of the Holy Spirit, which transforms our thinking. That's why the apostle Paul wrote, *"I pray that the eyes of your heart may be enlightened, so that you will know what is the hope of His calling, what are the riches of the glory of His inheritance in the saints, and what is the surpassing greatness of His power toward us who believe. These are in accordance with the working of the strength of His might"* (Ephesians 1:18-19).

Then, we should apply what we learn. Proverbs says we demonstrate fear of the Lord by hating evil and turning from it (3:7, 8:13); being humble and content (3:7, 15:16, 22:4); and living an upright life (14:2). These attitudes and behaviors glorify God, which results in a life of worship.

Proverbs also tells us that godly fear affects our lives in remarkable ways. Fear of the Lord prolongs life (10:27); gives us refuge and a fountain of life (14:26-27); provides instruction for wisdom (15:33); produces satisfying sleep (19:23); and offers riches, honor, and life (22:4). As such, godly fear is a gift of God's grace.

As His children, we don't live in fear of punishment, but in pursuit of pleasing our heavenly Father. Genuine reverence for God is demonstrated by how we think and live. How is your life marked by the attitudes and effects of godly fear? Remember, fear of the Lord is the beginning. We are always learning, always seeking, and always striving to know Him more.

Day 65

To Know Wisdom: A Fool's Game

"*Fools despise wisdom and instruction.*" Proverbs 1:7b

Occasionally acting foolish doesn't make one a fool. However, Proverbs clearly describes the person whose life is a fool's game. Throughout this book of wisdom, three different Hebrew words are translated, "fool." Today's verse isn't talking about the dimwitted or the ruthless fool. Rather, this fool is corrupt, morally perverted, and unreasonable.

In Proverbs, Solomon contrasts wise thinking and behavior with their foolish counterparts. The first part of Proverbs 1:7 says, "*The fear of the Lord is the beginning of knowledge.*" So, the fearless fool who "*despise[s] wisdom and instruction*" is unteachable, combative, and holds righteous instruction in contempt. People who despise wisdom and instruction aren't ignorant, they are arrogant. They are so full of themselves that there is no room for God.

They don't care Who God is or what He thinks. Furthermore, they pleasure in mocking those who do fear and obey the Lord. They love to debate petty things, refusing to discipline their tongues. Confronting them with godly truth only serves to embolden them, affirming their cause against godly fear and wisdom. The result is a life of futile pursuits. There is not enough pleasure, power, or profit in all the world to make them happy.

The psalmist was perplexed as he described these people to God in Psalm 73:11-12, *"They say, 'How does God know? And is there knowledge with the Most High?' Behold, these are the wicked; And always at ease, they have increased in wealth."*

What follows is a warning for those who despise wisdom and knowledge of God. *"When I pondered to understand this, it was troublesome in my sight until I came into the sanctuary of God; then I perceived their end. Surely You set them in slippery places; You cast them down to destruction. How they are destroyed in a moment! They are utterly swept away by sudden terrors!"* (Psalm 73:16-19).

Like the psalmist, we begin to understand the futility of such thinking by seeking God. Even as believers, we need to guard against foolish attitudes. Although you might not be combative toward God, do your words tend to display arrogance or pettiness? Would others describe you as unteachable or unreasonable? While these questions might anger a fool, wisdom leads us to repent of such harmful ways. We need to be careful; a fool's game results in a fool's pain.

Day 66

The Aim of Discipleship

"Go therefore and make disciples of all the nations, baptizing them in the name of the Father and the Son and the Holy Spirit, teaching them to observe all that I commanded you; and lo, I am with you always, even to the end of the age." Matthew 28:19-20

Today's passage gives the final instructions of Jesus, *"Go... and make disciples."* In order to fulfill the Great Commission, we need to answer two questions, "Who is a disciple?" And, "What is the aim of discipleship?"

To make disciples we must first *be* His disciples. Within the Great Commission, Jesus also describes His true disciples. First, they possess His Spirit, which is why Jesus said, *"I am with you always."* Next, they publicly identify with the death and resurrection of Christ through baptism. And they obey His commands and follow His teachings.

Sadly though, many professing believers don't pursue personal discipleship. But we fall short if we view the Great Commission as evangelism only. That's like rejoicing over the birth of a baby, then never teaching that child how to function in the world. The aim of discipleship is to develop a personal walk with the Lord that transforms us into His nature. This conformity to Jesus Christ is what identifies us as His followers.

Every Christ follower has the responsibility of disciple-making; showing others how to follow Jesus. The apostle Paul perfectly demonstrated the aim of discipleship when he said, *"Follow my example, as I follow the example of Christ"* (1 Corinthians 11:1 NIV). The Holy Spirit teaches, convicts, and comforts us from God's Word. We simply pass along what we've learned to someone else. That's discipleship.

So, if you've been saved and call yourself a Christian, are you following Him? His invitation remains, *"Come, follow Me"* (Matthew 4:19). How are you intentionally developing a personal walk with the Lord that increasingly transforms you into His nature? Salvation is a one-time experience. But biblical discipleship is the life-long pursuit of following Jesus Christ. And, you're commissioned to go and make other disciples.

Day 67

The Accountability of Discipleship

"All scripture is inspired by God and profitable for teaching, for reproof, for correction, for training in righteousness; so that the man of God may be adequate, equipped for every good work."
2 Timothy 3:16-17

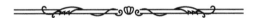

Last time, we said that the aim of discipleship is to develop a personal walk with the Lord that transforms us into His nature. Many evangelical churches emphasize the importance of personal discipleship, as well as meeting in discipleship groups. Sometimes though, the discussion can get off track. Verse 16 helps us examine the accountability of discipleship.

Meeting to discuss personal opinions or feelings about what we've read is fine for a book club, but somewhat dangerous when that book is the Bible. Part of being *"train(ed) in righteousness"* is submitting our opinions and feelings to the authority of God's Word. We come to erroneous conclusions when we're not accountable to Scripture — despite the sincerity of our group.

Jesus gives us an example of the accountability of discipleship. In Mark 8:27, He asked the disciples, *"Who do people say that I am?"* A few of them offered opinions they had heard. Then Jesus asked, *"But who do you say that I am?"* Peter replied, *"You are the Christ."* Jesus immediately confirmed Peter's answer without acknowledging the wrong opinions that had been shared.

Next, Mark's account tells us that Peter rebuked Jesus for saying that He must suffer rejection and die. Jesus then rebuked Peter, saying, *'Get behind Me, Satan; for you are not setting your mind on God's interest, but man's'"* (Mark 8:33). On the surface, it may seem that Jesus' response was harsh. But Peter's opinion was based on emotion rather than on the very words of Christ.

We, too, need to guard against interpreting Scripture by how we feel. We need to examine our emotions under the teaching, reproof, and correction of God's Word. Are you also willing to submit your personal interpretations of Scripture to God? Will you ask Him to show you what opinions need correction?

Pursuing a personal walk with the Lord that transforms us into His nature is easier with the encouragement of other believers. But as mature Christians in discipleship groups, we're accountable to guide discussions to the truth of God's Word. Remember, biblical discipleship is the result of continual submission to the Word of God.

Day 68

The Application of Discipleship

"All scripture is inspired by God and profitable for teaching, for reproof, for correction, for training in righteousness; so that the man of God may be adequate, equipped for every good work."
2 Timothy 3:16-17

The most common misunderstanding about discipleship is that it's all about how we think. While biblical thinking is key, we need to recognize the progression in discipleship. Our aim is transformation to the nature of Christ. Accountability to God's Word (v16) leads us to the application, *"equipped for every good work."* Growing disciples demonstrate the life of Christ in their thinking *and* doing. Many believers tend to focus on one or the other. But the apostle Paul links accountability to Scripture directly to the application of discipleship.

First, verse 17 doesn't say, "every good discussion or debate." It says, *"every good work."* Now, theological discussions are necessary, and can even be a good work. However, when they become the primary work, our focus is inward rather than on the lost. Neither should the work become primary. Meeting the physical needs of hurting people opens doors to share the Gospel, but we are not truly following Christ if we focus on good works without fulfilling our commission to make more disciples.

The disciples of the first century made a difference *in* the world because they were distinctively different *from* the world. Their relationship with Jesus transformed how they thought and what they did. Because they had the mind of Christ, they submitted to His Word and carried out His instructions. They lived in the fullness of the Holy Spirit to the point that they would rather die in obedience to Christ than live for anything less.

We see it in their treatment of fellow believers, their wholehearted devotion to the church, and their incredible enthusiasm for worshipping the Lord. It wasn't simply that they stopped doing the wrong things. They started doing the right things: encouraging, serving, and loving others.

The discipleship process hasn't changed. As we grow in our relationship with Jesus, our obedience to His Word and our love for others will increase. Because we have the mind of Christ, we fulfill God's purposes. As a result, everything we think and do brings glory to Jesus. After all, isn't that what discipleship is all about?

Day 69

Sacred Sexuality: Is God Anti-Sex?

"God blessed them; and God said to them, 'Be fruitful and multiply, and fill the earth...'" Genesis 1:28a

The sexual revolution of the 1960's caught Christians off guard. Music and movies began expressing new attitudes, promoting sex as just a physical act of pleasure. Confining sex to marriage was suddenly viewed as restrictive. The new mantra became "free love." Most churches only addressed the subject in a prohibitive way. As a result, God was perceived as a killjoy. So, fifty years later we're left with an important question. Is God anti-sex? To find the answer, we need to understand the purposes of sexuality.

First, God told Adam and Eve to have children, *"Be fruitful and multiply..."* He biologically designed them with sexuality and told them to express it with each other. Even though children aren't always the result, continuing the human race is one of the main reasons God created sex.

Then, in Genesis 2:24 we're told, *"For this reason a man shall leave his father and his mother, and be joined to his wife; and they shall become one flesh."* Sex unites a man and a woman physically, emotionally, and spiritually. Expressing our sexuality is designed as a way for a husband and wife to show affection and commitment to one another. In that context, sex promotes marital unity.

Finally, Proverbs 5:18-19 says, *"Let your fountain be blessed, and rejoice in the wife of your youth. As a loving hind and a graceful doe, let her breasts satisfy you at all times; be exhilarated always with her love."* Not only does God promote sex; He says it's meant to be enjoyable. Of course, seeking pleasure was at the core of the sexual revolution, but God-given sexuality is sacred. As such, it is designed to be enjoyed within the covenant relationship of marriage.

So, no, God is not anti-sex. He created sex to have both practical and pleasurable purposes. Talking about it is not only okay, it's necessary. Rather than just cursing the darkness, Christians need to share the light of truth. And the truth is, sex was God's idea. He is glorified when we honor His plan by recognizing the sacred nature of sexuality.

Day 70

Sacred Sexuality: Do Your Views About Marriage Reflect Your Faith?

"Marriage is to be held in honor among all, and the marriage bed is to be undefiled; for fornicators and adulterers God will judge." Hebrews 13:4

To say that marriage matters to God is a tremendous understatement. He established marriage as a covenant relationship in the Garden of Eden. Jesus performed His first miracle at a wedding ceremony. And the apostle Paul used marriage to describe the relationship between Christ and the Church. So, it's fitting that the writer of Hebrews includes marriage among practical ways to live out our faith. Today we'll consider the question, "Do your views about marriage reflect your faith?"

The first part of Hebrews 13:4 tells us to honor the institution of marriage. Honor begins by respecting God's design…one man and one woman for a lifetime. Many people contend that a certificate won't increase their commitment to one another. For believers, however, marriage vows are more than promises. It is a covenant relationship, reflecting God's covenant with us. It's often strong faith that helps a couple navigate difficult days. That's why a believer should only marry another believer (2 Corinthians 6:14).

Today's verse also instructs us to guard sexual intimacy within marriage. Being a faithful spouse is the foundation to fulfilling our marriage vows. This not only includes physical acts, but our thoughts and emotions as well. Also keep in mind that the purity of marriage begins long before vows are taken. Experiencing sex before marriage cheapens what God intended. Single believers live out their faith by choosing to abstain from sexual activity.

The fact that God promises to judge those who practice sexual immorality shows the value He places on marital intimacy. This exclusive relationship illustrates the purity Jesus expects in His bride, the Church (Ephesians 5:22-33). You might think it's too late. Maybe your marriage has suffered from infidelity, or you've strayed into promiscuity. Well, God also forgives and restores (John 4:7-30; 8:1-11). No person is beyond His reach and no marriage is too far gone for His help.

So, do your views about marriage reflect your faith? Will you choose to live out your faith by remembering that your God-given sexuality is sacred? The world's view of sex is nothing more than a cheap imitation of God's creation. When we value marriage as God does, and guard our sexuality, then we'll enjoy sex the way God intended.

Day 71

Sacred Sexuality: Why is Sex Outside of Marriage Harmful?

"Flee immorality. Every other sin that a man commits is outside the body, but the immoral man sins against his own body."
1 Corinthians 6:18

Our culture sends the message that casual sex is not a big deal. The apostle Paul addressed similar views in the city of Corinth. Why is sex outside of marriage harmful? Because sex *is* a big deal. Abusing our God-given sexuality is a sin against ourselves. Sex unites two people physically, emotionally, and spiritually. So, when it is pursued merely as recreation, it harms our entire being.

First, sexual sin harms us physically. Twenty million new cases of sexually transmitted diseases are reported every year. But disease is not the only physical consequence. As believers, the weight of unconfessed sin often shows up in our bodies. After committing adultery, King David cried out, *"Make me to hear joy and gladness, let the bones which You have broken rejoice"* (Psalm 51:8). Rebellion against God brought despair to the point that David's body ached.

Sex outside of marriage also harms us emotionally. God designed sex to be a lifetime bond within the covenant of marriage (Genesis 2:24). Two people may have a one-night stand, but both carry a lifelong memory. The impact of their shared experience affects their identity, security, and future relationships.

Finally, the spiritual harm of sexual immorality is grossly overlooked. 1 Corinthians 6 reminds believers that we are one with the Lord in spirit. Our bodies are the temple of the Holy Spirit and members of the body of Christ. The Lord does not suddenly abandon us when we act immorally. Paul boldly asks, *"Shall I then take away the members of Christ and make them members of a prostitute? May it never be!"* (1 Corinthians 6:15).

Everything about the way God created us is good. For instance, He gave us an appetite for food, which is both necessary and enjoyable. He also created sexual desires for marriage, but that doesn't mean sexual pleasure should be our chief pursuit. I love the way Warren Wiersbe puts it, "Sensuality is to sex what gluttony is to eating; both are sinful and both bring disastrous consequences."

Our culture would have you believe that sexual satisfaction is life's ultimate pleasure. In reality, pursuing sex outside of God's design harms your entire being. If you've allowed worldly ideas to affect how you think and live, then flee from it. When your chief pursuit is God, Himself, you'll find purpose, joy, contentment, and unimaginable peace.

Day 72

Sacred Sexuality: Can Believers Practice Sexual Sin?

"Now the deeds of the flesh are evident, which are: immorality, impurity, sensuality…those who practice such things will not inherit the kingdom of God." Galatians 5:19–21

Throughout this series we've established that God created sex exclusively for marriage. We've also discussed how harmful it is to pursue sexual pleasure outside of God's design. The problem is, many who call themselves Christians also participate in things that are immoral, impure, or sensual. So, can believers practice sexual sin and still be saved?

The word "practice" in Galatians 5:21 refers to a habitual lifestyle. Both Galatians 5 and 1 Corinthians 6 list sexual sin among behaviors of those outside of Christ. 1 Corinthians 6:11 goes on to say, *"Such were some of you; but you were washed, but you were sanctified, but you were justified in the name of the Lord Jesus Christ and in the Spirit of our God."*

That's why 2 Corinthians 5:17 says, *"Therefore if anyone is in Christ, he is a new creature; the old things passed away; behold, new things have come."* At the moment of salvation, we are pardoned, purchased, and possessed by Jesus Christ (1 Corinthians 6:19–20). If we have the Spirit of the living God within us, how can we continually practice rebellion without remorse?

So, what does it mean if you claim the name of Christ and aren't convicted by what God calls sin? Well, two possibilities come to mind: (1) you have a hardened heart; or (2) you are not really a Christian. Let's talk about these one at a time.

First, Christians can commit sexual sin, but not without the conviction of the Holy Spirit. The Lord may stop prompting a believer who continually ignores the Spirit. One of God's harshest disciplines is giving us what we think we want. The result can be a hard heart. That doesn't mean you lack sensitivity to others, but to God. Keep in mind, this includes sensual entertainment. How can we judge others then turn around and pay to watch similar behavior?

The other possibility is that you are not truly a follower of Christ. Consider 1 Thessalonians 4:3, 7-8, *"For this is the will of God, your sanctification; that is, that you abstain from sexual immorality...For God has not called us for the purpose of impurity, but in sanctification. So, he who rejects this is not rejecting man but the God who gives His Holy Spirit to you."* Sexual immorality not only violates God's will, it also demonstrates rejection of God Himself.

If you're a genuine believer who has fallen into the grip of sexual sin, then you possess the power to break free. Simply confess your sin to Jesus. Allow Him to live through you once again. If you are not a follower of Christ, God loves you and desires to make you new (2 Corinthians 5:17). He stands ready to forgive. Invite Jesus into your life by placing your trust in Him.

So, the question we should really ask isn't, "Can a Christian practice sin and be saved?" But rather, "Why would a follower of Christ choose to sin repeatedly when Jesus provides the grace and power not to?"

Day 73

Timely Advice: Be Strong

"You therefore, my son, be strong in the grace that is in Christ Jesus." 2 Timothy 2:1

Christianity faces numerous challenges today. Bible teaching is watered down, twisted, or disregarded altogether. Christians around the world suffer persecution for their faith. And new threats to Christian freedoms arise every day. No doubt, it's a difficult time to be a follower of Jesus. But many similar issues already existed in the first century. That's why Paul's encouragement to Timothy is still timely advice for 21st century Christians.

In 2 Timothy 2:1, Paul tells his young protégé to be strong in the grace of Christ. It's the same basic instructions he gave the church at Ephesus in Ephesians 6:10, *"Finally, be strong in the Lord and in the strength of His might."* You see, effective Christian service rests on God's performance, not on human skill or strength. Believers must rely on His might in order to be strong in the grace of Christ. This requires stepping out in faith to possess all that God's grace already provides.

First, we need a confident knowledge of God. Daniel 11:32 tells us, *"The people that know their God will display strength and take action."*

The more we know about God, the more it motivates and empowers us to act in His strength daily. Learning the names of God is a great way to begin. The Psalms reveal His nature by names such as, Mighty God, Lord of Host, God our Refuge, Rock, Deliverer, Defender, Healer, Helper, and Provider. As we grow in the truth of Who God is, we grow in faith as to what God does.

We also need a heart set on Christ. In Matthew 12:30, Jesus says, *"He who is not with Me is against Me; and he who does not gather with Me scatters."* A heart that is not intentionally set to know and serve the Lord defaults to thoughts and actions that do not please Him. Whereas, a heart set firmly on Christ never considers any option other than obedience to His Word. As the old hymn says, "Trust and obey, for there's no other way to be happy in Jesus, but to trust and obey."

So, when the Christian life seems difficult, remember Paul's timely advice. Be strong; not in your own strength or skills, but in His might. The Lord will enable you to do all that He commands. And His grace is sufficient for every challenge.

Day 74

Timely Advice: Entrust the Faithful

"The things which you have heard from me in the presence of many witnesses, entrust these to faithful men who will be able to teach others also." 2 Timothy 2:2

Many of us evaluate our faith based on God's faithfulness to us. Yet, we seldom examine whether or not God can count on us to be faithful servants. Can God trust you to pass on the truths of Scripture? Paul's guidance to young Timothy, to entrust the faithful, is still timely advice for believers today.

According to Hebrews 11:6, it's impossible to please God without faith. It's the key to the effectiveness of our prayers and our personal ministry. We'll never understand God's definition of faithfulness if we don't grasp how He evaluates our faith. The Bible speaks of little faith, no faith, dead faith, weak faith, futile faith, sincere faith, great faith, firm faith, precious faith, increasing faith, holy faith, and complete faith...just to name a few.

So, how should we measure our faith and faithfulness? First, by our love for God. Jesus made a very clear statement in John 14:15, *"If you love Me, you will keep my commandments."* God equates obedience with love. Our obedience is most consistent when our love for God burns hottest. So, we need to evaluate whether or not our obedience is motivated by genuine love for the Lord.

We can also measure our faith by our vision. *"For we walk by faith, not by sight"* (2 Corinthians 5:7). Faith is far from blind. It fixes our eyes on Jesus, the Author and Perfecter of faith. Intentional focus gives us His eternal perspective. Strong faith sees, thinks, and evaluates on the basis of His Word and His will. That way, we don't get trapped by temporary distractions that weaken our faith and hinder our faithfulness.

Finally, perseverance is a measure of our faith. *"We ourselves speak proudly of you among the churches of God for your perseverance and faith in the midst of all your persecutions and afflictions which you endure"* (2 Thessalonians 1:4). Perseverance is trusting God in such a way that our faith grows and deepens with every storm and every season of life.

So, what is the condition of your faith at present? Can God count on you as a faithful servant? If you want to be entrusted with passing God's truths to lost friends and family, then determine to be evaluated as one who lives faithfully.

Day 75

Timely Advice: Be Ready for Suffering

"Suffer hardship with me, as a good soldier of Christ Jesus."
2 Timothy 2:3

The idea of suffering hardship for one's faith is foreign to most American Christians. Yet, believers around the world suffer persecution regularly. The fact that Christian living entails continual warring against the forces of evil was not lost on the apostle Paul. After all, he was writing to Timothy from his own imprisonment. His advice rings just as true today as it did in the first century. If you follow Jesus, then be ready for suffering.

Like Timothy, we should have no illusions regarding following Christ. Being faithful to the truth inevitably leads to difficulties. Just ask those who come to faith in countries where conversion is punishable by imprisonment, beating, and even death. Still, many Christians continue to proclaim the Gospel against the constant threat of persecution.

In our own country, some reject and cut off Christian family members who are unwilling to compromise on God's Word. That's a form of suffering for one's faith. According to Paul, none of this should really surprise us. He compares our faithfulness to a soldier's service to his king.

Bible commentator William Barclay helps us understand the characteristics of a *"good soldier."* While on a campaign, a soldier is not involved in the ordinary business of life. All concentration is on serving. Early training conditions a soldier to obey commands without question. There may come a time when such instinctive obedience saves lives, including that of the soldier. Loyalty and sacrifice are a way of life. When a Roman soldier joined the army, he took an oath of loyalty to his emperor. As believers, we serve Jesus Christ. He deserves our loyalty through all the chances and changes of life, down even to the gates of death.

So, is your faith ready for suffering? Proclaiming the name of Jesus Christ is increasingly difficult in our country. How willing are you to stand on the truths of Scripture if it means rejection and hardship? Paul's advice remind us that following Christ is costly. Remember, the only kind of faith that has no suffering is one that demands no sacrifice.

Day 76

Timely Advice: Don't Get Entangled

"No soldier in active service entangles himself in the affairs of everyday life, so that he may please the one who enlisted him as a soldier." 2 Timothy 2:4

It seems like *"the affairs of everyday life"* increase with each generation. It would be interesting to know what came to the apostle Paul's mind when he used that phrase. Whatever it was, he warned Timothy that they were entanglements that could interfere with his service to the Lord. If that was true in the first century, then it's certainly timely advice for busy believers in the 21st century!

So, what exactly does it mean to be "entangled?" Well, it's the idea of becoming involved in an activity to the point of interference with other activities or objectives. Now, Paul doesn't mean that we should ignore our responsibilities. That wouldn't honor the Lord, either. Rather, his advice should cause us to be on the alert for the acceptable and good pleasures of life that can easily interfere with serving the Lord.

Avoiding entanglement is a frame of mind that largely determines what we do with our time and efforts. Since followers of Jesus Christ are primarily citizens of Heaven, then we should be busy with heavenly affairs. In other words, we should prioritize the eternal over the temporal.

Jim Elliot was a martyred missionary, and 2 Timothy 2:4 was his life verse. Before his death, Jim wrote in his journal, "He is no fool who gives up what he cannot keep to gain what he cannot lose." Jim Elliot had an eternal point of view, which allowed him to discern between the permanent rewards of Heaven and the passing pleasures of the world.

It has been said, "If you find yourself loving any pleasure better than your prayers, any book better than the Bible, any house better than the house of God, any table better than the Lord's table, any person better than Christ, any indulgence better than the hope of heaven—take alarm!" So, what about you? Is your time, energy, and affection given first to God for His purposes and glory? Or, does He get whatever is leftover? Just remember, when pleasing yourself takes priority over pleasing the Savior, it's a sure sign you are entangled.

Day 77

Giant Slayers are Offended by What Offends God

"For who is this uncircumcised Philistine, that he should taunt the armies of the living God?" 1 Samuel 17:26

People are so easily offended these days. And more times than not, beliefs and opinions that support a biblical world-view are quickly labeled as offensive in our culture. Yet many Christians remain silent when belligerent statements about God and Scripture are made. So, how easily should a Christian be offended; and by what? In today's passage, David the shepherd boy teaches us the first characteristic of becoming a giant slayer. We should be offended by what offends God.

Too often though, we're more like David's brothers and the ranks of Israel. They became so used to hearing Goliath's defiance of Israel's God that it didn't strike their ears the way it did David's. It was like, "Here comes this guy again with his usual anti-God rhetoric." The fact that he was big and intimidating kept them quiet and well behind the battle lines. David, on the other hand, was incensed by Goliath's disregard for the Lord. And, it caused him to act.

The more often we hear or see something, the more we become accustomed to it. Make no mistake, the media and entertainment industry intentionally treat the things of God with contempt. Their goal for decades has been to change the way our society thinks — and they have. Many times, believers pay to watch things that should actually anger us.

Christians have been playing defense for so long that we've gotten comfy behind the battle lines. But before we can face the giants of our culture, we need to once again be offended by what offends God. Like David, we need to step out in faith and say, "Who *is* this? How dare they talk about the living God that way!"

Think about the ways you've heard God's authority challenged this week. How have you seen a disregard for what God considers holy and sacred? Have the courage to step out in faith and act. Determine to not allow anything into your mind that is offensive to God. Would you watch that show or movie if Jesus was physically sitting next to you? The giants of our culture are big, loud, and well-equipped. It may seem as if all you have is a small stone. What good is that against a giant? Well, it's enough to make a difference somewhere when you trust it to God.

Day 78

Giant Slayers are not Easily Discouraged

"Now Eliab his oldest brother heard when he spoke to the men; and Eliab's anger burned against David and he said, 'Why have you come down? And with whom have you left those few sheep in the wilderness? I know your insolence and the wickedness of your heart; for you have come down in order to see the battle.'" 1 Samuel 17:28

Carrying out a God-given task isn't always easy. God's assignments often require great persistence. In order to battle the giants in our culture, we need to steadfastly overcome when difficulties arise. A closer look at today's passage teaches us an important principle: giant-slayers aren't easily discouraged.

Facing Goliath was a pivotal moment in David's life. God's plans for him were far greater than this shepherd boy could have imagined. But just as soon as the Lord stirred David to act against this God-defying giant, he was met with disapproval. As the oldest of eight brothers, Eliab was used to being the leader. God, however, chose David over all his brothers to be the next king of Israel. Although Samuel thought Eliab was the obvious choice, God knew he had a heart problem (1 Samuel 16:6-7).

It seems that Eliab's pride was injured, which kept him from being on board with God's plan. So what did David do? He simply turned from Eliab and found the answer he sought from someone else (1 Samuel 17:29-30). David was persistent to follow the guidance of the *"Spirit of the Lord"*, which came upon him when he was anointed by Samuel (16:13).

Like David, we need to consider the source of discouraging comments. Is a friend or family member trying to give godly counsel or warn you about consequences you may not have considered? Then it's wise to listen and pray before continuing. Remember, even unconstructive or pessimistic remarks might contain a grain of truth.

It can be difficult to discern when a challenge is God closing a door or if it's an obstacle we need to overcome. Accomplishing great things for the Lord comes by listening to the promptings of the Holy Spirit and operating in His power.

What discourages you from following through on a God-given task? If all it takes is words, then the anti-God giants in our culture will consume you. Don't allow someone else's lack of enthusiasm stop you from obeying God. Learning to overcome obstacles will strengthen your faith as well as your resolve to follow the Lord — no matter what.

Day 79

Giant Slayers Seize Opportunities

"David said to Saul, 'Let no man's heart fail on account of him; your servant will go and fight with this Philistine.'" 1 Samuel 17:32

Believers often see things within their church or community and think, "Someone should do something about that." Well, God might want you to be that someone! Young David shows us by example that giant slayers seize opportunities when they arise.

David was certainly surrounded by men who seemed better qualified and better equipped to fight Goliath — starting with his brother, Eliab, and King Saul! But the sight of this God-defying giant caused stronger, more experienced soldiers to lose the heart to fight. Even though Saul looked at David and saw only a boy, this boy had the faith of a giant-slayer. When the Lord prompted David to act, he didn't wait to be asked — he volunteered.

Now, imagine a different story. What if David had simply delivered the food to his brothers then returned home to tell his father the battlefront news? He would have done exactly what was expected of him, and he would have avoided the disagreement with Eliab. But he would also have missed the opportunity to serve the Lord in a mighty way. And keep in mind, God's name was glorified in the victory *because* David was not the obvious choice.

We allow opportunities to pass us by for a variety of reasons. We imagine other people are better qualified or have known the Lord longer. We can be fearful of the commitment or shortsighted regarding how God is working. Many times, however, we're simply selfish with our time and resources. The Lord often reveals an issue in order to set us in motion. Although it may seem overwhelming at first, if the Holy Spirit is prompting you to step up, then He will also guide you through the task.

Have you asked God to give you opportunities to serve Him or to tell someone about Him? Make a slight change in how you pray. Ask God to open your eyes, allowing you to see the opportunities that already surround you each and every day. Listen to the prompting of the Holy Spirit then step out in faith and seize the opportunity to serve. Who knows, you might even stop a God-defying giant along the way.

Day 80

Giant Slayers are Confident in the Lord's Faithfulness

"The Lord who delivered me from the paw of the lion and from the paw of the bear, He will deliver me from the hand of this Philistine." 1 Samuel 17:37

Faith is a spiritual muscle that grows stronger the more we use it. Each difficulty we face in God's strength is a faith-building exercise. Remember though, faith is only as strong as the person in whom it is placed. Today's passage teaches us that giant-slayers are confident in the Lord's faithfulness.

Why was young David so sure he could defeat Goliath? Well, this was not the first time the Lord had delivered him from great peril. He had experienced similar victories over both a lion and a bear, while watching his father's flock (1 Samuel 17:33-36). Still, David's confidence was not in his own abilities. It was obvious that the giant Philistine could overpower him, purely on a physical basis. But God doesn't calculate in the natural realm. Having relied on God's power in private battles gave David confidence in the Lord's faithfulness for this public battle.

We, too, can draw strength by looking back at the Lord's previous faithfulness. It's important to note that God's faithfulness is not measured by whether or not He acts according to our prayers. We usually ask Him to remove the challenge before we have to fully face it. The Lord could have kept the lion and the bear away from David's flock, but then he wouldn't have been prepared for this God-defying giant named Goliath.

God is faithful to walk beside us as we deal with each challenge. Relying on Him gives us strength, guidance, wisdom, and discernment. And, it exercises our faith for things to come. In what previous situation has God shown His faithfulness to you and to your family? How does looking back give you confidence to face today's difficulty?

Each time you rely on God's strength, you're developing giant-slaying faith. Thinking that way should change how you pray. Rather than asking God to take the problem away, trust in His ability to handle it. Rest in His faithfulness. Today's challenge belongs to the Lord; and so does the victory!

Day 81

Giant Slayers Don't Pretend to be Who They are Not

*"Then Saul clothed David with his garments and put
a bronze helmet on his head, and he clothed
him with armor...So David said to Saul,
'I cannot go with these, for I have not tested them.'
And David took them off." 1 Samuel 17:38-39*

When God presents us with a new or larger opportunity, we need to be careful not to dwell on how others would carry out the task. At first, we might even approach the job the way that a seemingly more qualified person would. Here's the problem; God didn't call someone else to that particular undertaking. David teaches us an important principle in today's passage. Giant slayers don't pretend to be who they are not.

When David volunteered to fight the giant Philistine, King Saul suited him in armor like the rest of his army wore. Verse 39 paints a humorous picture, *"David girded his sword over his armor and tried to walk."* The armor didn't help; it only incumbered him. David wasn't a soldier and couldn't successfully pretend to be one. He was a shepherd. So, he used the tools of a shepherd and the skills that had been developed by protecting his father's flock through the years.

We can accomplish what God has called us to do, using the spiritual gifts, talents, and skills that He's given us. He equips each of us with exactly what we need. Now, that's not to say we shouldn't prepare ourselves. The Lord may prompt you to pursue a specific path of preparation in order to enlarge your ministry for Him. Or like David, your preparation for greater ministry might come by faithfully fulfilling the role He's already given you.

While our paths of preparation can be similar, they are not identical. Ask yourself: 1) To what greater work is God calling me? 2) Am I comparing myself to someone else, and how is that hindering my obedience? 3) Which past experiences, natural talents, and spiritual gifts will help me to accomplish this task? 4) Do I need to pursue higher education or more information in order to fulfill this calling?

Yes, we need to be ready when God places the opportunity in front of us. Then we need to trust that He has prepared us to complete whatever assignment we're given. Remember, giant slayers don't pretend to be who they are not, because it only incumbers our work for the Lord.

Day 82

Giant Slayers See the Spiritual Battlefield

"Then David said to the Philistine, 'You come to me with a sword, a spear, and a javelin, but I come to you in the name of the LORD of hosts, the God of the armies of Israel, whom you have taunted.'"
1 Samuel 17:45

Our culture has become more and more contentious. A battle for traditional Christian values is at the core of many conflicts. The God-defying giants of our day are increasing in both size and number. Too often, we fail to see the spiritual battle and try to fight for a righteous cause in the flesh. In today's passage, David shows us that giant slayers see the spiritual battlefield.

On the surface, 1 Samuel 17 looks like Israel versus the Philistines; David versus Goliath; a slingshot versus a sword, a spear, and a javelin. Saul and Israel's army hadn't engaged because they were intimidated by an earthly enemy and earthly weapons. David, however, recognized the spiritual battlefield in front of him.

First, he knew the purpose for the battle, *"that all the earth may know that there is a God in Israel"* (v46). Now, the Lord is perfectly capable of defending His name. Although He could have opened the ground to swallow the entire Philistine army, God had a purpose for David's righteous anger. As word of the shepherd boy defeating the Philistine giant spread, so did the name of Israel's God.

Secondly, David knew this battle was actually *God* versus Goliath, *"the battle is the Lord's"* (v47). So, he relied on the power of the Lord's name. In Psalm 124:8, David wrote, *"Our help is in the name of the LORD, who made heaven and earth."* David was confident that the same God whose power created the heavens and the earth, would put the power in his sling to defeat this God-defying giant. He stepped out *"in the name of the LORD of hosts"* (NASB), *"the LORD Almighty"* (NIV), and *"the LORD of Heaven's Armies"* (NLT).

What stirs your righteous anger? Before you act, call on the name of the Lord. Fully submit your thoughts and attitudes to the Holy Spirit. Defeating the God-defying giants in our culture requires resisting the temptation to fight in the flesh. Ask God to show you how to step out in faith and take a stand for Him. The God who put the power in David's sling still rules the hosts of Heaven. So remember, *"Our help is in the name of the LORD"* — the battle is His.

Day 83

Giant Slayers Run Toward the Battle

"Then it happened when the Philistine rose and came and drew near to meet David, that David ran quickly toward the battle line to meet the Philistine." 1 Samuel 17:48

The God-defying giants in our culture don't just speak out against Christian values. They try to marginalize and silence followers of Jesus Christ altogether. As these giants have become more aggressive, many Christians have withdrawn; only vocalizing their biblical beliefs inside the safety of the church house. David shows us today that giant slayers don't shrink back when the heat is turned up; they run toward the battle. In order to help us effectively engage in spiritual warfare, let's reflect on David's example.

First, David knew what was at stake — the name of the Lord (v26). Every time Goliath taunted God's people, he was defying the one, true, living God. And it offended him. So, he seized the opportunity to take a stand for the Lord by taking on the God-defying giant (v32). It's one thing to be offended by all the anti-God, anti-Bible rhetoric in our culture; it's quite another thing to actually do something about it. How can you call other believers in your community into action? As you do, remember to speak and act in ways that elevate and honor the name of the Lord.

Next, David knew who was fighting the battle (v37). Because David's confidence was in God's faithfulness rather than his own abilities, he got rid of anything that would incumber him (vv38-40). Likewise, we're more likely to speak up for the Lord when we've spent time in His Word. We gain courage by reading accounts of His faithfulness to those who've gone before us, and by meditating on His promises to be faithful still. We also need time alone with God in prayer. Not only to ask for His strength, but also to confess any sin that would incumber our efforts or taint our testimony.

Have the God-defying giants of our day silenced you? Engaging our culture doesn't mean we have to argue and debate. It simply means that we speak and act when the Holy Spirit prompts us to do so. The courage to step up for a righteous cause requires stepping out in faith and running toward the battle.

Day 84

Why the Cross Still Matters: Substitution

"He made Him who knew no sin to be sin on our behalf, so that we might become the righteousness of God in Him." 2 Corinthians 5:21

Every person is born with a sin nature, making us enemies of God. Those who reject this idea see no need for a Savior and give no thought to what actually took place on the Cross. The Cross still matters because that's where God made a substitution on our behalf. Jesus was completely innocent when He went to the Cross. Yet, He took on the sins and guilt of the world.

The great evangelist Dwight L. Moody told the story of the young man who did not want to serve in Napoleon's army. So, when he was drafted a friend volunteered to go as his substitute. Sometime later, the surrogate was killed in battle.

Through a clerical error, however, the same young man was drafted again. "You can't take me," he told the startled officers. "I'm dead. I died on the battlefield." They argued that he was standing right in front of them. Still, he insisted they look to find the record of his death. Sure enough, there on the roll was the young man's name, with another name written beside it.

The case finally went to the emperor himself. After examining the evidence, Napoleon said, "Through a surrogate, this man has not only fought, but has died in his country's service. No man can die more than once, therefore the law has no claim on him."

Two thousand years ago, Jesus went to the Cross to die in our place. He became what He hated most in order to deliver those He loved most. And through Him our names are written in the Book of Life. The only person qualified to be our substitute did so willingly. Our salvation is legitimate because His name is written beside ours.

That's why the Cross still matters. Without His substitution we would be accountable for our sin before God the Father. Rejecting your need for a Savior doesn't change the truth. One day, you will stand before the Lord and the roll will be checked. Will your name be written there? Won't you accept His offer to be your substitute? He died once so that anyone who believes on Him will not have to die twice.

Day 85

Why the Cross Still Matters: Redemption

"Christ redeemed us from the curse of the Law, having become a curse for us—for it is written, 'Cursed is everyone who hangs on a tree.'" Galatians 3:13

Have you ever told a lie, taken something that didn't belong to you, or lost your temper? If so, then you're guilty of breaking the perfect standard required by God's Law. The penalty is eternal separation from God in Hell — where agony and sorrow never cease. That's why the Cross still matters. Jesus' willing sacrifice redeemed us from the guilt and curse of the Law.

By definition, redemption is regaining possession of something in exchange for payment. It's clearing a debt, which is exactly what Jesus did on the Cross. Without Christ we are all cursed and condemned to die, but His blood paid our penalty, clearing our sin debt and all its guilt.

The problem is, many people dismiss the Cross, believing their good deeds will save them. There are a couple of problems with this train of thought. First, we could never be good enough for long enough to earn our own redemption. Second, we would live in constant fear of not having enough good works to outweigh the bad.

There's a great story that helps us understand redemption. A little boy built a sailboat, took it to the lake, and hoped it would sail. Sure enough, the boat went rippling along the waves and was soon out of his reach. He hoped the breeze would shift, bringing the boat back to him. Instead, he watched it go farther away until it was gone.

Sometime later, the little boy saw his boat in the window of a second-hand store. So, he went in, picked it up, and said, "This is my boat." The owner of the shop said, "That's my boat. I bought it from someone." The boy showed him the marks where he had hammered and filed, evidence that he had, indeed, made this little boat. The man said, "I'm sorry. If you want it, you have to buy it."

So, the boy worked hard and saved his pennies until he had enough money to buy the little boat back. As he left the store he said, "You're my boat twice; first because I made you, and second because I bought you!"

That's the picture of redemption! The very God who created us, bought us back in an amazing act of grace. Salvation cannot be earned. It is God's free gift through Jesus. So yes, the Cross still matters!

Day 86

Why the Cross Still Matters: Identification

"I have been crucified with Christ; and it is no longer I who live, but Christ lives in me; and the life which I now live in the flesh I live by faith in the Son of God, who loved me and gave Himself up for me."
Galatians 2:20

In talking about why the Cross matters, we've established that Jesus died as our substitute, redeeming us from the penalty of sin. Sadly, that's where many believers stop. Today, the apostle Paul reveals the importance of our identification with the death, burial, and resurrection of Christ. That's what Paul meant when he wrote, *"I have been crucified with Christ; and it is no longer I who live, but Christ lives in me."*

Paul realized that his old, sinful self was nailed to that cross. As followers of Jesus, we need the same realization. Although we weren't there 2000 years ago, we died and were buried with Christ through faith. Romans 6 states this reality over and over again: *"We died to sin"* (v2), *"We have been baptized into His death"* (v3), *"buried into death"* (v4), *"united with Him in the likeness of His death"* (v5), and *"our old self was crucified with Him"* (v6).

Jesus, Himself, instructed believers to live each day in this reality. In Luke 9:23 He says, *"If anyone wishes to come after Me, he must deny himself, take up his cross daily and follow Me."* Denying self means yielding your personal desires and agenda to God's will. Identification with the death of Christ is essential to authentic discipleship. German pastor and theologian, Dietrich Bonhoeffer, put it this way, "When Christ calls a man, He bids him come and die."

Uniting with Jesus in death means we can also identify with His life. Romans 6:11 tells us that we are, *"alive to God in Christ Jesus."* By agreeing with God that our old self is dead and buried with Christ, we can enjoy the victory of His resurrection in everyday life.

Will you consider the death of Jesus on the Cross as your death to self? Or, are you still living by your own agenda? Yield those desires completely to the risen Lord. Then you will have the identifying marks of His disciples: submission, service, and sacrifice. That's why the Cross still matters.

Day 87

Why the Cross Still Matters: Emancipation

*"...though you were slaves of sin, you became obedient from the heart...
having been freed from sin, you became slaves of righteousness."*
Romans 6:17-18

Jesus' death paid for our freedom, but we need to understand what Christian freedom entails. Jesus not only paid the penalty for our sin, He also set us free from the power of sin. So, the Cross is our emancipation from slavery to sin.

Before salvation we had no defense. We were controlled by the sinful nature with which we were born. But sin's power was broken on the Cross. Romans 6:14 declares, *"sin shall not be master over you."* Although our ability to sin was not completely destroyed, Jesus conquered its power over us. So, if we sin as believers it's because we choose to sin, not because we're powerless to overcome the temptation.

Still, Christian freedom is often misunderstood. It doesn't mean we do anything we want because forgiveness is available through grace. When we identify with the death of Christ, as we discussed last time, we willingly submit to Him as our new Master. Through obedience to Christ we choose to become *"slaves of righteousness."*

Galatians 5:24 tells us, *"Now those who belong to Christ Jesus have crucified the flesh with its passions and desires."* Our freedom from sin's power and from a personal agenda enables us to be what He created us to be — bearers of His image.

It's impossible to break the power of sin on your own. And according to Scripture, you don't have to try. Jesus went to the Cross to win your freedom from the penalty and power of sin.

Are you enjoying the freedom found in Christ? If so, then you can sing the old hymn, "At the cross, at the cross where I first saw the light, and the burdens of my heart rolled away, it was there by faith I received my sight, and now I am happy all the day!"

Day 88

How to Resist the Devil

"Submit therefore to God. Resist the devil and he will flee from you."
James 4:7

"Not today, devil!" is a popular saying printed on everything from t-shirts to coffee mugs. While we can applaud the sentiment, believers need to seek biblical truth over pithy sayings. So, what does Scripture say about resisting the devil?

The Bible declares that sin no longer has authority over the life of those who are born-again. Romans 6:14 clearly states, *"For sin shall not be master over you, for you are not under law but under grace."* This doesn't mean, however, that Satan leaves us alone and no longer targets us with temptation. He still presents us with worldly desires that appeal to our flesh.

A critical element missing in much of mainline preaching is the role of fully submitting to God in order to effectively overcome the devil's attacks. Satan has no fear of us. More importantly, we have no defense against him in and of ourselves. That's why James 4:7 instructs believers to, *"Submit therefore to God. Resist the devil and he will flee from you."*

Before we can say, "No" to the devil, we must say, "Yes" to God! It is Jesus who gives us the victory. He fights our battles. He shields us from the arrows and assaults of the enemy. Claiming the promise of victory without submitting to the person of victory is like having a gun with no bullets. Before you can say, "Not today devil" with any real confidence, you have to say, "Yes today God" with a sincere and submissive heart.

Day 89

Truth Can Withstand Examination

"The first to plead his case seems right, until another comes and examines him." Proverbs 18:17

Today's verse, like many of the Proverbs, presents us with a commonsense scenario. There are two sides to every story. People often share different versions of the truth when accusations arise. So, how do we know which to believe? Well, truth can withstand examination. Let's look at three tests we can implement to help discern what's true.

First, employ the test of God's Word. Are the accusers acting biblically? Did they attack publicly before confronting privately? Are they acting in anger, pride, or jealousy? Remember, accusation is a primary weapon of Satan. Sometimes, it's all he needs to discredit a believer's testimony. So, if witnesses and evidence don't support the accusation, we can reasonably question its truth.

Next, use the test of time. Impulsive conclusions often create more confusion than clarity. Time, on the other hand, allows tempers to cool down so rational conversations can take place. While talking and listening takes time, the reward is accuracy and truth.

Finally, draw on the test of personal relationships. Because believers are accountable to one another, we should build relationships with mutual accountability in mind. So, what do those closest to the people involved say about the situation? Be careful not to assume that anyone close to the accused is simply lying. Once we do that we're no longer in pursuit of the truth. And truth matters more opinion.

Christians should protect the integrity of the innocent, regardless of ideology differences. Finger pointing and false accusations cause unnecessary pain and heartache. Even when the allegations turn out to be true, believers need to respond with patience and compassion. Truth can withstand examination. So, before taking sides, give God's Word, time, and accountability an opportunity to work.

Day 90

Grateful for the Cross

"But may it never be that I would boast, except in the cross of our Lord Jesus Christ, through which the world has been crucified to me, and I to the world." Galatians 6:14

The Cross of Jesus Christ takes away any grounds we might use to exalt ourselves. However, it gives us every reason to boast of Jesus and His great sacrifice. Are you grateful for the Cross? It is the bridge spanning the chasm of condemnation that kept us separated from God. Only He could take an instrument of condemnation, guilt, and shame and turn it into a symbol of love, liberty, and life.

Are you grateful for the love shown on the Cross? *"But God demonstrates His own love toward us, in that while we were yet sinners, Christ died for us"* (Romans 5:8). Love compelled God to send Jesus to the Cross. And love compelled Jesus to give His life on the Cross. This love was not stimulated by mankind's recognition of our sinful condition or our need for a Savior. God's sacrificial love came from Heaven before people on Earth even knew they were condemned.

Are you grateful for the liberty that comes from the Cross? *"So if the Son makes you free, you will be free indeed"* (John 8:36). By paying the penalty for our sins, Jesus set us free from eternal sorrow and separation from Him. The Cross also gives us liberty in this life. Our freedom is not to do as we wish; but to please God with how we live.

This mindset stems from gratitude for the blood of Jesus, which washes away our sin and gives us access to the throne of God.

Are you grateful for the life made possible by the Cross? *"For if we have become united with Him in the likeness of His death, certainly we shall also be in the likeness of His resurrection,"* (Romans 6:5). Through salvation, our old nature is crucified with Christ. And through His resurrection we are regenerated — not merely reformed. So, the life of Christ lives in and through us, which makes fellowship with God possible.

We don't deserve the love displayed on the Cross. Nor can we earn the liberty Christ's sacrifice affords. Our only qualification is the shed blood of Jesus Christ. Of all the things for which we are thankful, we should be most grateful for the Cross. So, let's live today in service of our Savior and Lord!

CPSIA information can be obtained
at www.ICGtesting.com
Printed in the USA
FSHW020753250221